Colin Challen is Labour MP for Morley & Rothwell. Prior to his election to Parliament in 2001, he was a local Labour party organiser. Before that he was a self-employed printer and publisher, having started a small business after leaving university in 1982. Before going to Hull University as a mature student, he was a postman and served in the Royal Air Force. A member of the House of Commons Environmental Audit Select Committee, he has presented several bills in Parliament, including bills to promote personal carbon rationing and the international climate change framework Contraction and Convergence. In addition, he launched and is a founder member of, the All Party Parliamentary Group on Climate Change which he chairs. His other publications are: *The Quarrelsome Quill, Hull's Radical Press from 1832* (Hull, 1984); *In Defence of the Party: The Secret State, the Conservative Party and dirty tricks* (with Mike Hughes) (Leeds, 1996); *Save As You Travel: New directions in mutual ownership* (Wakefield, 1999); *The Price of Power: the secret funding of the Conservative Party* (London, 1998). He was editor, *Labour Organiser* 1997 to 2001.

too little, too late

the politics of climate change

Colin Challen MP

First published in Great Britain 2009 by Picnic Publishing
PO Box 5222, Hove BN52 9LP

Copyright © Colin Challen

The right of Colin Challen to be identified as the author of this work has
been asserted by him in accordance with the Copyright, Designs & Patents
Act, 1988.

A catalogue record for this book is available from the British Library.

ISBN: 9780956037008

Printed and bound in Great Britain by RPM Digital

contents

—

prologue: I left my memory stick in Nairobi and I'm shaking my head because I've got a headache

What follows is a morning in the life of a United Nations Framework Convention on Climate Change (UNFCCC) conference – the annual Conference of the Parties (COP) and/or MOP – Meeting of the Parties to the Kyoto Protocol. The tortuous processes of the UNFCCC are a mystery to many who attend their meetings, and this is partly because what happens on the floor of the conference hall in the time honoured traditions of political fixing is often predetermined by caucus and cabal beforehand. So, the most important voices at the conference may not be those of single countries, but of groups of countries that go by the name 'European Union,' 'Umbrella Group' or 'G77 plus China.' The United States is one of the few countries which at least as late as 2007 could still try to stand aloof and almost single-handedly seek to shape events. In his very brief account of the Kyoto conference in 1997 – which the British media at least hailed as a significant success brought about by himself – John Prescott wrote in his memoirs of the "incredibly complex" nature of the discussions that eventually agreed to a 5% cut in greenhouse gas emissions on the part of the developed world. But what really took place might more realistically be described as the 'race to be second' as the Tyndall Centre for Climate Research characterised the workings of a later UNFCCC conference. A race that is, to get somebody else to do the right thing and then hopefully to get away with doing less oneself.

It is unlikely that many high flyers would want to dally too long with the arm wrestling over the agenda that took place in the plenary Subsidiary Body for Implementation (SBI) meeting on the first Tuesday morning at the Bali COP/MOP in 2007. I reproduce in full my notes of a two hour ping pong match, in which perhaps tellingly the Chinese (and the G77) finally overcame developed world opposition to some modest proposal about how technology transfer should be discussed in future UNFCCC proceedings. What follows will give you an idea of the sometimes tortured nature of UNFCCC talks. The issue was how to ensure that technology transfer should be given greater emphasis in the UNFCCC SBI process. The discussion took place in a session of the SBI.

> The meeting started 25 minutes late (at 10.25am) due to the late arrival of the G77 Chair (Pakistan) – the prior G77 caucus meeting must have taken longer than planned formulating their position. Pakistan speaks on behalf of the whole G77. Once underway, the Chair (of the SBI) pointed out – it was just possible to discern this in his fog of jargon – that there appeared to be an 'unresolved issue' at yesterday's full COP meeting to set the conference agenda. Pakistan agreed. Saudi Arabia backed Pakistan. It seems they believed the COP had made a clear decision – to include "Development and transfer of technology" as a separate item on today's agenda. We pick the story up at 10.40am: (Errors and omissions: this is from my much condensed handwritten notes, so falls well short of Hansard standards!)

Chair: (*Reads note from COP Secretariat*) This is not a new item, it's on the agenda anyway. It's merely a question of resolving a misunderstanding. Does Pakistan agree?

Pakistan: It's going back on an understanding. We want a decision now – take the matter now.

China: We want a decision now before we start the rest of the agenda. The memo contradicts yesterday's decision.

Saudi Arabia: Like the Chinese, English is not our mother tongue, so misunderstanding is possible, so it should be a separate item under SBI.

Chair: Originally we did not want new items. Thought that was agreed. Does the G77 want a new item?

Pakistan: English not our mother tongue either. Want SBI to do something it hadn't done earlier. Item should be discussed.

Chair: English is not my mother tongue also. It was understood that the request was not for an additional item. There is a procedure to follow. So how do we proceed, we can turn to it if the house considers it necessary.

Saudi Arabia: Wanted it as a separate item.

Bulgaria: (*Pushed their button by mistake.*)

Philippines: Support G77. It is on the record.

Chair: Question to the G77: are you proposing a new item?

Pakistan: You're putting words into my mouth. I'm discomforted by the Chair – we already had an understanding – the COP decision was clear.

Chair: No desire to put words into your mouth. But want to be clear – I had a clear impression there was a demand for a new item. (*Chair then proposes a new item "Development and Transfer of Technology" to be added to SBI agenda.*)

Egypt: Supports item before treatment of any other.

Chair: Are you for the Chair's proposal?

Ghana: It's already on COP agenda. COP decided SBI and SBSTA should consider it *(N.B. It's already being considered by SBSTA)*

Japan: What is being proposed? We propose an adjournment to consider the issue.

US: We've gone in a slightly different direction. On behalf of the Umbrella Group we need clarification of Chair's proposal. What would be considered? Technology has always been considered in SBSTA. It's appropriate there. No need for duplication *(in SBI)* SBI Chair should undertake informal consideration with G77 and others.

Portugal (President of EU speaking on EU's behalf): EU keen to engage. COP decided SBI could consider it. Several ways of doing it. Further consultations would be welcome.

China: Proposal in regard to Chair's proposal: your job is to execute COP proposal. Disappointing if some developed countries negotiate in bad faith. Not a single delegate opposed G77 when call for item to be considered by both SBSTA and SBI. Not sure why they raise the issue in this room – is it because the press aren't here? Press were in COP but there they were silent. Should speak openly! We're here to exercise decisions of COP.

Chair: Is it my understanding nobody questions validity of COP decision to refer item to SBI? There are questions of ambiguity about our procedure, not its substance. How to deal with it – the COP president merely wanted it discussed, not necessarily as a separate item. Let's have some informal consultation between 1pm and 2pm.

Pakistan: No interventions were made opposed to making of COP decision. It's a sensitive subject. SBSTA is a technical body. See no need for informals, there's a readiness for this item in SBI.

Chair: I see three more requests to speak – the Chair is in your hands.

China: Supportive of G77 Chair. G77/China were very co-operative yesterday. You (to Chair) have received the instruction of the COP President, it is unnecessary to have informal discussions. You should have this as a formal agenda item for SBI and form a contact group.

Chair: Thank you very much my dear Chinese colleague. I suppose I have alluded to this, an established procedure for a new agenda item. The President of COP did not give a clear instruction that it should be discussed as a fresh agenda item.

US: We question parties' intent on shifting agenda items – don't want contradictory positions. Let's have an informal discussion.

Saudi Arabia: This could have been resolved by now – want transcript of yesterday's COP, let's look at it for five minutes. We cannot continue unless we immediately resolve the issue. If we start now to trick each other what chance for a road map?

Ghana: You have clear instructions from COP President from yesterday. It is obviously a separate item.

Gambia: Supports G77. There was no opposition from other groups yesterday. Perhaps they thought about it later. And now there's a misunderstanding.

Chair: Verbatim is on its way to the podium. Will read it out.

Australia: (Notice to speak withdrawn)

Tanzania: Support G77. Instructions of COP were clear – it's no longer just a SBSTA issue.

Bangladesh: Should be guided by COP decision – should be adhered to.

China: As Ghana said you have clear instructions from COP President or your job is impossible. We are cheated by negative approaches. Our ancestors were bullied by those countries. Keep to what we have said, we cannot agree and then change agreement later. The international community has high expectations of Bali. This issue is dear to our hearts. If you do not have clear instructions then adjourn the meeting and rescue COP immediately, but at an informal.

Chair: I'm still waiting for the verbatim.

Mali: (spoke in French)

Chair: Merci. *(Chair calls Cameroon)*

Canada: You mean Canada, Chair.

Chair: You can speak in French too, if you want.

Canada: We're all parties interested in this issue. The discretion does rest with the SBI. We are interested in the subject matter the G77 have discussed. Let's take up the informal discussions.

Chair: Here's the text, from the President of COP, four paragraphs only. G77 called for it to be a substantive issue in SBI, SBI can take it over from SBSTA. Can it be agreed? No objections? *(Signs of dissent in the hall.)*

Pakistan: Your task is easier now. To US/Canada – what we want is what I said yesterday, don't think there is any need to wait any longer. We want to send a positive signal to the world, we will take important decisions, we don't want blocks to achieving our objectives. Let's have no more questions, it's clarified. Let's go out and have a cup of coffee – but it's our hope that the vulnerable states who need technical support, adaptation and finance get the help they need. We are positive in spirit *(applause)*.

Chair: The verbatim is quite clear. I proposed to go to informal discussion, that was rejected, therefore if you agree we can have this item now.

Pakistan: We agree it should now be taken.

Chair: I just did. It's now a proposal by the Chair for a new item.

Pakistan: We are clear that this is a COP decision. If that is what you mean, and nobody objected, we are happy to proceed.

Chair: I suppose it is clear it is left to my discretion as Chair of SBI. If you agree, the G77 will tell us about the substance – no objection?

Japan: I lost my memory stick in Nairobi, so often have no memory. But I do have short-term memory. The verbatim shocked me. I do not understand this question, so want informal discussion. Still need to discuss how to proceed in the best way with this item. Need to discuss what the substance of this item may be. Whether Annex I or II countries, still need to discuss other important issues in SBI. What could be the substance of this agenda item?

Chair: It appears the list *(of speakers)* is getting longer and longer.

China: (point of order to Chair) It is not your position to make a proposal but to execute the COP decision. Need clarification if SBI is seeking to overturn COP. Withdraw your proposal.

Chair: The question is not for the SBI Chair. The decision of COP was to refer consideration of importance of technology transfer to SBI. How this is to be done is left to the SBI – including the Chair. My proposal was to formalise the referral of the matter by the COP. The President and the memo are clear enough on a separate agenda item. I have listened to you. We need a common understanding.

Pakistan: (point of order) Increasingly frustrated. Three times we've made it clear, the agenda item is moved. Our request is that you should follow the order of COP.

Chair: (consults colleague) My proposal "Development and transfer of technology" is exactly the same as the COP13 item.

Pakistan: We request adoption of the agenda now.

Chair: I wish I could – some colleagues are in dissent, shaking their heads in the wrong direction. That is why I ask for an informal discussion, coming back at 3pm for the Chair to exercise the gavel.

Pakistan: I'm shaking my head because I've got a headache. When agenda is adopted we will go to informals.

Chair: I can see everyone in a wide panoramic view. Am I in a position to adopt a new agenda item? Colleagues must raise their hands. Still not able to exercise the gavel, some colleagues protest the new agenda item.

China: This is really unnecessary – the President has already gavelled, the COP has already gavelled. Use your discretion to execute the COP decision.

Chair: There's a subtle difference here. Was it really sent as an agenda item? What is referred to is a discussion of the matter, but not necessarily as an agenda item. I'm just looking for an appropriate way of discussing it. It was merely a matter of referral.

China: (point of order) A great pity we're not able to translate a COP decision into action. Will this postpone climate change? We repeat, put it on the agenda. Let's proceed with what COP has decided.

Chair: I'm sure this is educational.

Portugal: (point of order) There is no doubt about the concerns this issue raises. We call for an adjournment of 10 minutes.

Chair: OK – if you really mean 10 minutes.

Session adjourned at 12.20pm, restarted 12.30pm

Chair: Hopefully we're now in a position to come to closure. We may have to rely on legal advice – the Chair couldn't come to a definite decision.

Legal Advisor: It does appear that the COP decided that the item should be referred to SBI as well as SBSTA. COP has the power to do so. The item is formally part of the SBI agenda. SBI should discuss the scope of such discussions and when it wants to discuss it.

Japan: Sorry for speaking again and again and thanks to the legal advisor, I have another question of clarification: based on the COP decision does SBI have to have it as a separate item?

UK: (pushed button by mistake)

Nigeria: Nothing to discuss, it's clarified and closed, there's no need to continue, the issue is on the agenda.

Portugal: We go along with the legal advisor.

Chair: Is it everybody's understanding that the item is on the agenda of SBI 27? *Exercises the gavel followed by emollient remarks.*

The Chair's seeming indecision seems heavily weighted towards the developed world. China is assertive – perhaps feeling it now exercises unassailable influence in the developing world (billions spent in aid and development in Africa, a new deep water port in Pakistan, etc.); the US is outnumbered but has to be listened to (although as a speaker said at a different meeting, who does the US Federal government representative represent these days? Certainly not America); the EU plays its hand as a listening broker. Two hours of this stuff, but at least the item is now on the agenda of SBI! I suspect it will be a long time before it's translated into action. Conclusion: the mother tongue of COP is oft tied, but to old hands of Labour Party conferences, it's a doddle.) A media report of this debate quoted Indonesian negotiator Salman Al Farisi saying "It is a breakthrough in the sense that developing countries can now hope for more immediate transfer of technology from developed countries as the issue is now being discussed under the convention's subsidiary body for implementation"

– as opposed to the subsidiary body for scientific and technical advice (SBSTA). The developing countries have their hopes up that something will happen.

introduction

So when the reality of our impotence dawns, would any politician dare order genuinely painful and real sacrifices for no certain benefit? Would the millions of 'super-rich' give up their yachts, mansions, super-cars and hugely destructive lifestyles? Would politicians sacrifice their pensions and live modestly? Would ordinary consumers even stop eating meat and coveting luxury? Would most of them even bother to wear winter clothes indoors in wintertime?

Dr Stephen Wozniak (public interest campaigner)[1]

The quotation above is taken from an article called Politicians Cannot Solve Climate Change (Even if They Tried). It presents the conundrum of the politics of climate change in a very stark light – a kind of damned if you do and damned if you don't world where both trying and not trying are equally as bad. It's like we have to change more than just the system which has created this problem, we have to recalibrate our very being, away from the 'perennially greedy, breeding' species that we are. Wozniak compares our society to a pyramid sales system, which can only support the unsustainable demands of today by introducing a greater pool of resource we can dip into tomorrow. He likens it to the way that we pay our pensions, which needs an ever increasing workforce to keep the payments up, recession or no. Politicians seem to have little or no control over this and indeed their policies and those of financial institutions have perversely focused on short term returns whilst nominally promoting the idea that we should all live into ripe old age.

If I shared the view (which has at least some obvious merit in the climate change context) that politicians are powerless to shape events or even come up with rational responses to events, then I think I must have wasted a good portion of my working life. But self renunciation is not a cure. Self analysis may be. Climate change means that politicians have to submit their long cherished beliefs to a challenging examination. Climate change is not about muddling through, as we have done in human conflicts past, or when social change happened by hit and miss. We can't say 'we'll give this a go and if that doesn't work we'll try something else' as if we had all the time in the world to correct our errors. The cumulative errors that we have already made call for a response which is unprecedented and has to be informed by an analysis which decisively breaks with the past. The 'pay later' culture of society has to stop. What if we had to live within our ecological and financial means today, and not borrow from the future? What if all our plans had to internalise that single thought? It would be a big step, but still not big enough. We have already borrowed too much from the future, we have to add a restorative element too. In Biblical terms (as an atheist I can nevertheless admire some of the Bible's secular wisdom) we could take as a model of restoration that part of the otherwise detestable Leviticus where it speaks of allowing the land to lie fallow for one out of every seven years. We have a society which is losing the concept that it needs to rest. At the UN Bali climate change conference in 2007, the Indonesian Tourism and Culture Minister had the temerity to suggest that the world should be allowed to 'rest' for at least one day of the year, like a Day of Silence or the Hindu Nyepi. According to the Jakarta Post 'It is estimated that during Nyepi, when Balinese Hindus refrain from conducting any activities and no motorised vehicles or flights are in operation, some 20,000 tonnes of emissions could be reduced.' The Minister, Jero Wacik said "By conducting the ritual, we at least stop using electricity, motorised vehicles, air conditioners and factory machinery for at least one day" but "there was not a single response from foreign participants. Maybe we have to fight for this idea locally first."[2] Perhaps Minister Wacik has not yet learnt that 24/7 production on a 'just in time' basis is our creed, and it allows no time for reflection as is so obvious in the way that our 24/7 media presents politics. So whilst countless political leaders have now said that we must radically change the way we do things, in the political domain it remains largely business as usual.

Do politicians see themselves as leaders of society or prisoners of society? It should be a choice, not a dilemma. It must be one of the strangest characteristics of political life that in order to be successful one must on the one hand be a suitable subject for hero worship, but on the other hand be a humble servant of the people. The master/servant relationship usually cannot be combined in the same personality, but that's what democracy expects. Indeed, in the way our haphazard democracy has developed, it's precisely what it enables at least as a mirage, and the development of this mirage is one of the great conceits of our democracy. It would do no harm to remind ourselves again and again that 'western democracy' is still in an early and experimental stage of its development. What we now tend to consider to be a fully matured system with all its checks and balances has barely been around for as long as the lifetime of today's oldest living person. The evidence we use to demonstrate the robustness of our inheritance – and therefore its assumed superiority - is of very recent origin. Most of us would probably cite the defeat of fascism in the Second World War as a great if not the greatest triumph of democracy, and the first real proof of its strength. This assessment is often tied to an analysis which heralds the Americans' involvement in the war as the defining turning point and necessarily has little regard to the contribution made by Stalin's dictatorship in defeating Hitler. Yet the most objective way of characterising the Allies' victory would be purely as a military and even more prosaically as a logistical victory, rather than a victory of the liberal democratic system. But such a statement will no doubt seem counter-intuitive to generations brought up to believe that the democrat's pen is mightier than the dictator's sword, even if the pen was wielded by Churchill when he was drafting his speeches.

Where does the power to change things really lie? Since the blessings of liberty are now increasingly understood to mean consumerist liberties, we in the developed world will continue to have a justification for enjoying what we will from the persisting inequalities of wealth between the north and the exploited south, stripping the planet's resources as if they not only belonged to the minority but were also limitless. In the words of the United States National Security Strategy, a key US objective is to "Ignite a new era of global economic growth through free markets and free trade." What difference might it make if this strategy said instead that we will "Create a new era of global democratic growth through tolerance, understanding and a fair and sustainable distribution of wealth?"

The Canadian writer John Ralston Saul wrote:

"Those who believe that democracy issued from the womb of the marketplace have a tendency to link freedom of speech to capitalism. George Bush [senior], for example, in his inaugural address spoke of how "a more just and prosperous life for men on earth" was accomplished through "free markets, free speech and free elections." The order given to the three freedoms is astonishing from the mouth of a man assuming the chief responsibility for the exercise of the American constitution. His suggested sequence of freedoms is an historical and contemporary fiction. The world is filled today, as it has often been in the past, with nations that embrace free markets, close censorship and false or no elections. Singapore and China spring to mind. And the more complete these markets, the tighter the controls become on the other two freedoms."[3]

The words of the US constitution which Ralston Saul alludes to are its very first words: "We the people . . ." and that is the authority for the rest. But the purpose of free speech and free elections now appears much more overtly to legitimise the outcomes and the whole practice of free markets; indeed the current model of electioneering has itself acquired the language of the business model, with the marketing and packaging of policies increasingly the norm. The oft reviled 'focus groups' are but one example of this. Their purpose is to eliminate or at least minimise the electorate's 'cognitive dissonance,' or the difference between their expectations and their actual experience. In other words, the public role of the politician is increasingly to 'keep the dream alive.' That dream is contagious, and anyone who questions the grounds on which it can be sustained is at best a spoilsport or at worst a sandal wearing denialist who can only afford the choice of rejecting rampant materialism by virtue of living in a comparatively wealthy society. That's a form of solidarity with the poor which pales against the solidarity the global business model offers, a model which could be characterised as 'the devil has all the best tunes.' The business model of 'solidarity' is not ideological (we are meant to believe) but is only concerned with creating and administering to people's wants. Here is an expression of it:

> It's also incorrect to assume that the poor are too concerned with fulfilling their basic needs to 'waste' money on nonessential goods. In fact, the poor often do buy 'luxury' items. In the Mumbai shantytown of Dharavi, for example, 85% of households own a television set, 75% own a pressure cooker and a mixer, 56% own a gas stove, and 21% have telephones. That's because buying a house in Mumbai, for most people at the bottom of the pyramid, is not a realistic option. Neither is getting access to running water. They accept that reality, and rather than saving for a rainy day, they spend their income on things they can get now that improve the quality of their lives.[4]

The authors go on to say that there is a common misconception (amongst businessmen) that goods sold to the poor must be cheap – on the contrary, they can be more expensive because the poor do not have trade, transport or communications advantages that richer people enjoy, which means for example that bulk buying is denied to them. In other words, the poor are losers in the market place. Never mind that they do not have running water (except through holes in their shanty roofs, perhaps) just so long as they can watch TV in order to live 'the dream.' And how are all these 'luxury' purchases to be paid for? Through free trade with the already rich, under a set of rules which have collectively been defined by the already rich.

Is it imaginable that this model is about to change? That it can be changed through the agency of human intervention, rather than a climate change catastrophe? It is not at all clear to me that it is. Perhaps if our representative democracy had had more time to mature, rather than mutate into the consumerist democracy it has become, things would look rosier. We have fallen into the trap of thinking that a solution to climate change can be delivered 'just in time,' that it can somehow fit into our election timetables and economic cycles, and even then perhaps not the current timetable or cycle, but the next.

I do not attempt in this book to advise on what steps the reader should take to reduce their carbon footprint. I assume that anyone interested in the politics of climate change may by now have passed the point of realising that changing to energy saving light bulbs and not purchasing four wheel drives are good things to do (although I acknowledge that energy saving lightbulbs may have health side effects, particularly for pregnant women). There are lots of books which explain the practical steps that people should take, and the last time I searched on the internet for 'carbon calculator' Google brought up 448,000 hits. There is an abundance of advice on how to reduce your carbon footprint, and the government's $ActOnCO_2$ campaign is probably as good a starting place as any.

Yet tellingly amongst the top three hits of my Google search, there was an ExxonMobil website. What on earth were they doing there? Who, seeking a measurement tool to help them reduce their carbon dioxide emissions needs to be directed to ExxonMobil's home page merely to be told: "By 2030, experts predict that the world will require about 40 per cent more energy than it did in 2005. Growth in developing countries will drive most of this increase, but energy demand is expected to increase in the United States, too"?[5]

There is a mass of contradictions embedded in Exxon's short statement. An unstated concern for the developing world's hunger for energy, which will help them out of poverty meets head-on the likelihood of catastrophic climate change, ready to undo many of the GDP-growth benefits of using fossil fuels. And although the only way we may be able to convince the developing world that they need to sign up to a meaningful global climate change framework is by demonstrating how we are cutting our own energy use, well actually our 'experts' advise otherwise – even in the technologically superior United States 'energy demand is expected to rise too.' So let's provide for it!

Perhaps Exxon's presence under 'carbon calculators' is actually a subversive webmaster's subliminal attempt to make people even angrier in the knowledge that within the global political-industrial nexus there remains a huge reluctance to give the problem of climate change the serious treatment it requires. It is clear that the experts Exxon rely on work on the same assumptions as those who have the power to change things do and are so reluctant or incapable of changing. Wielding real power in this context may mean sharing it, or even – heaven forefend – yielding it to others to build a consensus, a common cause.

Since one of the subjects I deal with in this book is cross party consensus, it is beholden upon me to try to be impartial judging the climate change performance of the different parties, but since I am a Labour MP the reader may occasionally find hints of partisanship creeping through. If that is the case I imagine it will be more than compensated for by the fact that the party which has held office since 1997 is necessarily the one whose record will be subjected to the most critical scrutiny in this book. I am led to a number of uncomfortable conclusions, which reflect my view that we – Labour – have not done anything like enough in government to match our rhetoric. But this does not mean that the opposition can take the moral high ground since they can still exercise a lot of influence, and the way that they choose to do so impacts greatly on the government's perception of what it can do – I almost said 'get away with.' That is the greatest lesson to be drawn from the fuel protests of 2000. It is also a moot point whether the opposition parties, principally the Conservatives would have performed any better. The dominant ethos that drives both the Labour and Conservative Parties, namely their devotion to market solutions, imposes on both the same constraints.

If all our traditional political constraints could be accorded their proper subservience to informed scientific consensus, then I might just feel able to join the optimist camp on climate change, that is those who see how radical action now may just pull us through with something like an evens chance of success. But I am not yet ready to make that leap into the optimists' camp, though it is absolutely worth working for. As things stand, we're more likely to be stuffed and I would recommend readers take up James Lovelock's gloomy prognosis in The Revenge of Gaia. I suppose then, after we've adjusted to our new circumstances, a degree of optimism could be rekindled, recalibrated to the reality beyond today's short sighted politics.

Colin Challen
2009

Notes

1. Politicians Cannot Solve Climate Change (Even if They Tried) Newsletter of Offwell Environment Link January 2008 http://seered.co.uk/offwell_climate_change.doc
2. *Jakarta Post* 5th December 2007
3. John Ralston Saul, *The Unconscious Civilisation*, Anansi, Toronto, 1995 p46
4. *"Serving the World's Poor, Profitably"*, C.K. Prahalad and Allen Hammond, *Harvard Business Review*, September 2002
5. http://www.exxonmobil.com/Corporate/news_opeds_20080731_investing2.aspx

1

the phases of war
and the coming storm

Why, this is hell, nor am I out of it

The Tragical History of the Life and Death of Doctor Faustus,
Christopher Marlowe, sc. III

Winston Churchill began The Gathering Storm, the first
volume of his history of the Second World War by describing
its theme as "How the English-speaking peoples through their
unwisdom, carelessness and good nature allowed the wicked
to rearm." [1] Without much alteration this discomforting theme
could easily sum up the tendencies of our age in response to
climate change. For 'English-speaking', read developed world;
for 'good nature' read 'faith in markets' (although there must
be many valid alternatives to the latter suggestion); and for 'the
wicked to rearm' read 'a perilous future to emerge.' When he
came to writing his memoirs in the late 1940s Churchill chose
to include in The Gathering Storm an example of his writing
from the late 1920s, penned well before others had woken up to
the danger of another conflict. He had written earlier:

> Mankind has never been in this position before. Without having improved appreciably in virtue or enjoying wiser guidance, it has got into its hands for the first time the tools by which it can unfailingly accomplish its own extermination. That is the point in human destinies to which all the glories and toils of men have at last led them. They would do well to pause and ponder upon their new responsibilities. Death stands at attention, obedient, expectant, ready to serve, ready to shear away the peoples en masse; ready, if called on, to pulverise, without hope of repair, what is left of civilisation.[2]

That passage was originally published on January 1st, 1929, and was no doubt revisited to show his readership 20 years later the enduring quality of the author's perspicacity. In 1929 there were plenty of events available (as eighty years later) to marginalise forebodings of bigger and longer-term threats. In October 1929 Wall Street crashed. Then (as now) economic woes interceded to grab the attention of Presidents and Prime Ministers. The ex-corporal Adolf Hitler merited but a single paragraph in the 1929 edition of Encyclopedia Britannica – he was merely noted as a "Bavarian politician." So who would be concerned by Churchill's warnings? He was listened to respectfully if sometimes begrudgingly by his colleagues in power, but they saw their duty as little more than to reassure the public that everything was being done that had to be done, and nobody should worry too much about our defences – everything was under control. Deference to authority was called for, then as it is now.

Leaders in today's society have to choose their words carefully to describe the scale of the threat posed by climate change. Churchill's warnings were not welcome in that earlier period of calm reflection known as the roaring twenties; today, after the longest period of sustained economic growth on record, what aspirant to power would want to emulate Churchill's example? Despite a clamour for him to do so Al Gore, possibly the most celebrated politician of 2007, declined to run for the US presidency. Perhaps he knew that his dire warnings of the impacts of climate change, whilst making him popular amongst parts of the 'commentariat' would not enamour him to large sections of an electorate concerned about their material wellbeing. In a deepening recession, Barack Obama overcame this difficulty not least by emphasising how new 'green' technologies could lift the U.S. out of a manufacturing doom and create millions of new jobs.

The Archbishop of Canterbury, Dr Rowan Williams, as thoughtful and erudite as he is has nevertheless found his words on climate change as likely to offend as to endear. When he said that political leaders would 'face a heavy responsibility towards God' if they didn't tackle climate change many thought he was speaking out of turn. He told Radio 4's Today programme "Nobody likes talking about governmental coercion in this respect - whether it is speed limits or anything else. Nobody, for that matter, likes talking about enforceable international protocols, and yet, unless there is a real change in attitude, we have to contemplate these very unwelcome possibilities if we want the global economy not to collapse and millions, billions, of people not to die. I think it's a profoundly immoral policy and lifestyle that doesn't consider those people who don't happen to share the present moment with us, who will be there in the future."[3] The responsibility for millions or billions dying, being laid at our door? Was he accusing us of genocide, merely because we haven't turned our central heating down by one degree or bought an energy saving lightbulb? How out of touch is the occupant of such a modest home as Lambeth Palace? Of course what Williams was saying (regardless of any belief in God) was that our lifestyle really does come at an environmental cost and there is actually not enough said about that outside of environmentalist circles. All he sought in pointing this out was, to paraphrase Churchill 'that we pause and ponder on our new responsibilities.'

The great military theorist, Carl von Clausewitz said that 'war is the continuation of politics by other means.' If so, then now we have a dual problem. The first is that the language we use has been pacified. It is no longer acceptable - least of all in a consumer society - to describe our political condition in the terms laid out by Archbishop Williams or his fellow bishops.[4] We struggle to make any connection between what we consume and its consequences. The second problem flows naturally: we become ever more separated from reality. Even the purely military wars which we have engaged in have been designed as far as possible not to expose our forces to danger, hence the increased use of high-altitude bombing and civilian losses. New technology permitting wars eventually will be made as close to virtual reality as possible, conducted from a safe distance with robots and drones undertaking the dangerous tasks.

War, genocide, climate change: how do we determine our location in the development of these phenomena in order to be better equipped to control and then eradicate them? The inter-war experience illustrates some, perhaps all of the major stages of the political continuum which concludes with a result, or at least 'closure.' And with 'closure' we should of course remember that as one door closes, another door opens – the completion of the Second World War naturally seemed to mark the start of the

Cold War. The four phases of the Second World War period – starting say from 1929, when Churchill wrote one of his earlier warnings – to 1945, can be defined as denial, appeasement, phoney war and total war. Without a proposition there can be no denial; appeasement is the awkward experience when conflicting desires demand to be met; phoney war is the period of shock which follows when appeasement devours itself – and total war is the complete immersion in solving the problem.

In this context it is not so easy to identify when the Second World War itself actually started, its gestation being more than one phase in that continuum. One correct date might be the 3rd of September, 1939 when British Prime Minister Neville Chamberlain formally declared war on Nazi Germany, following Germany's invasion of Poland on the 1st September. For the Czechs perhaps the war could be said to have started even sooner, with their annexation into Hitler's hegemony earlier in 1939. Or had the war started when Hitler retook the Rhineland in 1936? For the Americans, it might be the 7th December 1941, a date which President Roosevelt said "would live in infamy." Clearly, Chamberlain's historic humiliation on the 3rd September was in many ways no more than a political inevitability, the outcome of a protracted process – but it left his reputation, perhaps wrongly remembered 'in infamy' since there were many culprits, some of whom would not be able to recognise themselves a such and who were subsequently rehabilitated into the establishment's bosom of wisdom.

Now it seems we have entered a new era of war - the so-called 'war on terror' and we have a new date to play with: 9/11, complete with vivid images that will forever remind us precisely where we were on that fateful day in 2001 when the planes crashed into the twin towers. No doubt historians will consider that date, important as it is no more than a punctuation mark in a narrative which traces its beginnings to earlier periods and events.

If there were ever to be a 'war on climate change' (and I'm not yet sure there will be, regardless of whether one approves of the language) it would be very hard to actually pin point any dates of significant commencement. Here is a 'war' which emerged as a theory largely confined to a handful of scientists, and one which has gathered pace only in the face of public indifference, political insouciance and all round ignorance. Many still deny that any 'war' effort is required, that focussing on climate change is a significant error which will stifle development and so lead to the impoverishment of human fulfilment. But the sceptics have found it harder and harder to explain away the growing mountain of evidence that has confirmed or exceeded the climate change modellers' predictions. That evidence of course shows that the causes of this 'war' were grounded in the Industrial Revolution and the belief which sprung from it that industrial growth, i.e. GDP growth could be had without reference to any resource and particularly a fossil fuel straightjacket.

This interest in dates lies in trying to determine at what stage we're at in the fight against climate change. Having often used the war metaphor to describe the struggle we're engaged in whether we like it or not, I know that to many it is distasteful at best and possibly self-defeating at worst. But this insistence on likening the challenge of climate change to total war is not entirely confined to the fringes of political discourse. The European Union's Environment Commissioner Stavros Dimas described the challenge of climate change thus:

> As the scientific evidence accumulates it is clear that the fight against climate change is much more than a battle. It

is a world war that will last for many years and probably for many generations. Damaged economies, refugees, political instability and the loss of life are typically the results of war. But they will also be the results of unchecked climate change. It is like a war because to reduce emissions something very like a war economy is needed. All sectors, transport, energy, agriculture and foreign policy must work closely together to meet a common objective. And it is a world war because every country in the world will be affected by the results of climate change – although it will be the poorest who are hit hardest.[5]

Most senior politicians are not yet prepared to use this kind of language (and from the appropriate language one may hope the appropriate actions will follow). They and the general public are at various earlier stages of engagement – or disengagement. Perhaps Commissioner Dimas's words will sound to some as a little too histrionic. No doubt he would not be grateful for any suggestion that his words are akin to those of some increasingly anxious latter-day Churchill, but few others have spoken so forcefully.

But as the real-life Churchill was taking the reins of power in 1940, even then the sense of urgency, the sense of threat was absent, right in the heart of government. Clive Ponting wrote an excellent book called 1940: Myth and Reality which showed the Establishment of the day taking a more insouciant approach to the war than received wisdom would normally suggest. Ponting wrote:

If pre-war habits in high society continued virtually unchanged in 1940, so did other ways of life in the government, society at large and the armed forces. When Colville [the Prime Minister's private secretary] joined the staff at No. 10 in October 1939, he was shocked to find that work started at the 'disgustingly early hour' of 9.30. All-out war for national survival, however, did not alter practices elsewhere. Until November 1940 the Foreign Office began work at 11 a.m. and at the Ministry of Economic Warfare Hugh Dalton had to issue special instructions that staff were to be at their desks by 10 a.m. after one civil servant did not arrive in time for one of Dalton's meetings at 10.30 [6]

I would concede that the hours in the Foreign Office may now have changed, and I am sure that if we had a Ministry of Economic Warfare (or better still, a Ministry of Climate Change Warfare) its first ministerial meetings or at least phone calls might start before breakfast. But an early start must not obscure the fact that we are still – as they were then – more prepared to hope for something turning up to solve our problems than actually stripping away our comfortable routines. Then, something 'turning up' meant either the United States actively joining the war or a peace deal with Hitler, which some senior British politicians still thought possible. Now, in the 'war' against climate change, something 'turning up' still heavily depends on the United States – ending its neutrality on climate change – or perhaps through some curious and highly unlikely osmosis, all of us in the developed world changing our behaviour overnight.

Perhaps we are approaching the end of the denial phase, the first of the four phases characterising the gestation and maturation of the Second World War, and which are now clearly replicated in the evolution of today's much greater challenge. But as we shall see we are not entirely out of the denial phase yet, since the debate about climate change has so far been mainly about whether if one accepts it is happening one also believes it is anthropogenic in causation. That question has largely been scientific and has largely been answered amongst scientists, although a small and vociferous minority remain unconvinced. The really big question of whether the denial phase is over lies with the public and has most definitely not yet been substantially settled – as opposed to being merely canvassed in opinion polls. This is the real sceptic's battleground – in the political domain not the scientific one - although some politicians will milk any continuing dissent in the scientific domain for all it is worth. Hence, in the debate on the Climate Change Bill which took place in the House of Commons on the 9th June 2008, we find this not untypical interpretation of a minority scientific view being transformed into a seemingly conclusive argument for political inaction by Conservative MP John Maples:

Until a couple of months ago, I was happily riding this consensus and basically accepted the received wisdom. I thought that it was probably being exaggerated a bit, but then people usually do that in making a case. However, I then made the mistake of reading a few books and quite a lot of analysis, particularly of the Stern report. That has led me to a couple of conclusions that trouble me a lot. I do not believe that the science is anything like as settled as the proponents of the Bill are making out. In fact, the scientists hedge their predictions with an awful lot of qualifications and maybes that those who invoke them often omit. The science is a bit like medicine in the 1850s. The scientists are scratching the surface of something that they do not really understand, but no doubt will. They are probably on to apocalyptic visions that we have heard set out. [7]

Waiting for 'certainty' in science is a mug's game, and of course we would not have the medical cures we have to today if every doubt had to be banished first. We must rely on our reasonably formed instincts. Should we clear the hurdle of denial, there will then be (and already is – there is no clear delineation between the first three phases of this evolutionary process) an appeasement phase, followed by a phoney war phase. Following the phoney war comes – in Dimas's words as well as mine, total war – a clear transition emerges at this stage to something new, which is so unequivocal, it can best be described as a life and death struggle which calls on every sinew of effort, all the blood, sweat and tears, as Churchill might say. When that point is reached, there is no going back. At the present time, with international negotiations grinding on and endless government consultations appearing, there are still plenty of opportunities for equivocation and indecision.

We may well be passing through the messy border between denial and appeasement. In some countries there are plenty of signs of appeasement – the Chinese, prompted by their country's severe environmental degradation have undoubtedly understood that much needs to be done. They are one of the world's largest markets for renewable energy technologies, but China remains a vastly greater market for fossil fuels, particularly coal and increasingly of course, oil. This could be described as a state of appeasement, trying to ameliorate a problem one is nevertheless decisively doing nothing to stop. In contrast in the UK and the EU a phoney war has begun – with the setting of targets which might go some of the way to sorting the problem out but whose performance has yet to be proven. Witness the creation of the world's first multi-country carbon emissions trading scheme, the EU ETS. Although the first phase of the ETS was utterly ineffective, it nevertheless forms the centrepiece of many a high flown piece of political rhetoric and helps politicians glide like swans through one international conference after another with their heads held high, even though their graceful motion is not due to very much co-ordination beneath the surface. Theirs is often a new kind of perpetual motion, what the German SPD MP and renewable energy activist, Hermann Scheer has described as 'internationally talking, nationally postponing.' [8] This perpetual motion machine will only stop when it is recognised that the last phase of the conflict has begun. When President Bush wanted a war in Iraq no resource was spared even though it can be argued (in the language of the IPCC in a different context) that with a 90% degree of certainty, there were no weapons of mass destruction. No resources were spared – or it seems will be spared in the future on the Iraq war – given that one estimate puts the total cost of that war at $3 trillion.[9] There was far less certainty about Saddam Hussein's WMD than there is now about climate change, but by comparison the commitment is invisible.

How much 'international talking' needs to be conducted before we achieve an effective climate change solution is anybody's guess. Here we can return to the question of dates. Perhaps the first of these was the 'Earth Summit' held in 1992 in Rio de Janeiro, a conference which set up the United Nations Convention on Climate Change (UNFCCC). Perhaps the last date will be in December in Copenhagen, 2009 where the 15th conference of the parties to the UNFCCC will be held, with the task of finalising an agreement to follow the Kyoto Protocol.[10] Another date also comes to mind. This is some day in 2015, by which time the Intergovernmental Panel on Climate Change

(IPCC) has said global greenhouse gas emissions must peak and begin to fall if we are to avoid catastrophic climate change. Listening to the debate on climate change one could be forgiven for feeling that the IPCC is falsely encouraging us imagine we have a breathing space, in order to get things absolutely perfect, right down to crossing the t's and dotting the i's. We should remember that climate change is a process which pays little heed to human calendars and all our deadlines are in a very real sense artificial.

What makes matters worse is that our mortgage with the climate is heavily frontloaded – what we are prepared to pay now to sort the matter out will have exponentially greater impacts than dealing with the problem in equal steps over the long-term. For many non-scientists, the approach to climate change seemed at first to be a case of doing a little bit every year in a way that we need barely notice, and this would deliver the result we want. But as more is understood about the climate and ecosystems, it is becoming increasingly obvious that such a gentle, linear path to future success is far from guaranteed. The terms 'positive feedbacks' and 'carbon sink failures' suggest something rather more ominous, but in the main such issues have not yet been factored into the political discourse on climate change.[11] Partly this reflects the considerable uncertainty about them. Like lightning, we know enough about these phenomena that they are likely to occur, it's just that we can never tell for sure when. Positive feedbacks and carbon sink failures suggest non-linear, drastic known unkowns in our models both scientific and political, so are almost impossible to plan for in the discreet, predictive way that our present systems are designed for. How easy is it to plan a secure financial future when at any time you may be made redundant, your redundancy insurance company goes bust and your parents get dementia all at the same time? It could happen, but we assume that horrible things usually happen just to other people. Positive feedbacks and carbon sink failure is the nightmare we'd rather not dwell on. That is almost certainly going to be a huge mistake, but it will not have been the first.

The IPCC published its fourth assessment report of the science of climate change in 2007. The IPCC process is one of reviewing others' work, rather than itself carrying out original research – each assessment report is four years in the making, and involves reviewing and collating studies of the science of climate change and forming a consensus view of the impacts. The process inevitably has its detractors – there are undoubtedly those who demur from some of the conclusions of studies that may be included and find the consensual process artificial. Sceptics point to counter evidence which they say disproves any link between climate change and human activity – for them one counter example represents a fatal blow to the whole theory. For them, the IPCC is more concerned with obtaining 'political correctness' through consensus (a concept allegedly inimical to scientific method) than being honest and fair. This desire for 'political correctness' in part stems from a perception that governments are more willing to fund academic projects which subscribe to the majority view than to those which do not. Needless to say, such an accusation might not withstand too much scrutiny, if the federal administration of the United States were to be cited as one such government. There is ample evidence to suggest that scientists Bush's government did not approve of were more likely to be pilloried for espousing climate change propositions. Dr James Hansen, of NASA's Goddard Space Institute is perhaps the most prominent example.[12] Other cases were examined by US Congressional hearings by the House Oversight Committee in 2007 which examined the "Censorship of Science." It heard from a number of scientists that the Bush administration had "engaged in hyper-controlling strategies for the management of information" which led to the suppression of information, "anticipatory self-censorship," monitoring of "all interviews either in person or on the phone," "forcing scientists to change their data, editing scientific documents to alter their conclusions, distributing inaccurate science based information" and tellingly "budgetary cuts."[13] The power of this political response should not be underestimated when refuting sceptics' claims that that somehow climate change scientists have had a free run. The political resistance – not confined solely to the US - has rarely manifested itself in some grand Popperian dialectic modelled on 'conjecture and refutation' but rather the character attack. A little piece of forgotten history which might concern sceptics of the IPCC's output is that Bush – perhaps the world's leading sceptic - was influential in securing the appointment of what he assumed would be a retardant influence as the head of the IPCC. Working on the advice of ExxonMobil, Bush's administration moved to replace a known climate change champion with his own (wrongly assumed) 'yes' man. This was how the matter was reported at the time:

> ExxonMobil has been allowed to veto the United States government's selection of who will head the prestigious scientific panel that monitors global warming. Dr. Robert Watson, the highly respected leader of the Inter-Governmental Panel on Climate Change, was blackballed in a memo to the White House from the nation's largest oil company. The memo had its effect last Friday, when Dr. Watson lost his

bid for re-election after the administration threw its weight behind the "let's drag our feet" candidate, Dr. Rajendra Pachauri of New Delhi, who is known for his virulent anti-American statements.[14]

Exxon's memo, from its Washington lobbyist Randy Randol may or may not have reached the Oval Office, but certainly former Vice President Al Gore was concerned enough to assume that the damage could be laid at the Administration's door. The memo charged Bob Watson with giving a 'sneak preview' of the IPCC's Third Assessment Report (TAR) saying his comments to the press "blied his real intent, which was to get media coverage of his views before there was a chance fro the process to challenge his personal agenda." Watson appeared in Randoll's estimation to be part of a cunning exercise, on the very day of Bush's inauguration, to stymie Bush's freedom to wreck things: "The U.S. was represented by Clinton/Gore carry-overs with aggressive agendas."[15]

The 'let's drag our feet' jibe was Gore's, but did not quite square with an earlier call of Pachauri's for a boycott of American goods which caused pollution – such as ExxonMobil's products. But Exxon's memo makes clear how strongly they felt current IPPC chair Bob Watson was abusing his position to push a 'personal' agenda, which we can only assume made him the greater of two evils. In environmental circles, the election of Dr Pachauri initially caused dismay. But over the years, that response has evaporated since if it became clear that Dr Pachauri was never in any way a climate change sceptic, he has now become one of the world's leading exponents of the seriousness of the problem, and indeed it was perhaps with some irony that he on behalf of the IPCC received the joint Nobel Peace Prize in

Oslo in November, 2007 alongside none other than Al Gore.

At the other end of the scale, the IPCC has plenty of dissenters who find its consensual approach a road to conservatism, who say that in order to achieve a consensus it has to exclude studies which show the situation to be more serious than previously thought. Such studies by their very nature tend to be more recent and so have not yet had time to be submitted to the full four year peer review process. Some of these studies are concerned with positive feedbacks and carbon sink failures – the potential 'non-linear' impacts of climate change, such as the polar albedo effect, the melting of permafrost and consequent methane gas releases (20 times more powerful than CO_2) or the dieback of tropical rainforests – which have not so far been factored into standard predictions of an incremental trajectory of climate change. By their very nature, non-linear events are unpredictable. The translation of that area of research into any attempt at socio-economic modelling is naturally going to be very difficult, and runs counter to our political culture which imagines a smooth, fully integrated pathways into the future of our dreams. The very nature of this unpredictability also has the consequence of placing natural obstacles in the way of convincing people that climate change is real. At the time of writing in 2008 some attention has been paid to a probable downturn in temperature, possibly over a ten year period before it rises significantly again.[16] Combining such a cycle with a downturn in the economy, then the appetite for taking radical political action on climate change alters fundamentally for the worse, a subject we shall return to in a later chapter, but it effectively illustrates that moving from the denial to appeasement phase is not necessarily going to be a simple one-way forward motion.

The presumption of this author – and this will not come as a surprise if you have read thus far – is that the science is correct – or in the words of the Royal Society is "sufficiently sound to make us highly confident that greenhouse gas emissions are causing global warming."[17] The real question is to what level this warming effect will increase the temperature and what impacts that will have. The relationship between greenhouse gases and temperature clearly has many complexities – not all greenhouse gases operate in the same way and of course the sum of human knowledge about these processes is far from complete – if completeness were ever possible. But from what we do know, estimates can be made of the range of probabilities. Hence Malte Meinshausen (of the Swiss Federal Institute of Technology (ETH Zurich) Environmental Physics) produced a table of likely temperature changes given different concentrations of CO_2eq (carbon dioxide equivalent) in the atmosphere:

"The probability of exceeding 2° C warming above pre-industrial levels in equilibrium for different CO_2 equivalence stabilisation levels. Upper bound, mean and lower bound are given for the set of eleven analysed climate sensitivity PDFs" [18]

CO_2eq stabilisation level (ppm)	350	400	450	475	500	550	600	650	700	750
Upper Bound (%)	31	57	78	90	96	99	100	100	100	100
Mean (%)	7	28	54	64	71	82	88	92	94	96
Lower Bound (%)	0	8	26	38	48	63	74	82	87	90

This analysis shows, for example, that a CO_2eq. concentration of 550 parts per million (ppm) in the atmosphere has at least a 63% chance of increasing global warming of a level greater than 2°C. But the upper range of CO_2 ppm which is still mainly under active consideration in the formulation of climate change mitigation policy is 550ppm. Recent commentary suggests that level should be much lower. James Hansen for example now argues "If humanity wants to preserve a climate resembling that in which civilisation developed, then the palaeoclimate evidence and ongoing climate change suggest CO_2 must be reduced from its current level to between 300-350ppm." Hansen said of where we are today:

Arid subtropical climate zones are expanding poleward. Already an average expansion of about 250 miles has occurred, affecting the southern United States, the Mediterranean region, Australia and southern Africa. Forest fires and drying-up of lakes will increase further unless carbon dioxide growth is halted and reversed. Mountain glaciers are the source of fresh water for hundreds of millions of people. These glaciers are receding world-wide, in the Himalayas, Andes and Rocky Mountains. They will disappear, leaving their rivers as trickles in late summer and fall, unless the growth of carbon dioxide is reversed. Coral reefs, the rainforest of the ocean, are home for one-third of the species in the sea. Coral reefs are under stress for several reasons, including warming of the ocean, but especially because of ocean acidification, a direct effect of added carbon dioxide. Ocean life dependent on carbonate shells and skeletons is threatened by dissolution as the ocean becomes more acid. Such phenomena, including the instability of Arctic sea ice and the great ice sheets at today's carbon dioxide amount, show that we have already gone too far. We must draw down atmospheric carbon dioxide to preserve the planet we know. A level of no more than 350 ppm is still feasible, with the help of reforestation and improved agricultural practices, but just barely –time is running out.[19]

At levels over 500ppm the probability of moving towards a temperature increase of between 4°C and 5°C becomes more likely. Such a change might seem neither here nor there to some people (some who should know better say that people in different regions of the world happily live in climates greatly different from the rest, or that we have adapted to living in warmer city environments, so why worry?), and many in northern latitudes may welcome – at least at first – the possibility of warmer weather. More wine will be made in England, and an end to the traditional wet English summer spring to mind as commonly held opinions about the benefits of climate change in a U.K. context. Such parochialism could prove to be the undoing of effective policy-making. The destructive impacts of climate change in a globalised world will be felt all around the world as they strike. These impacts will seriously exacerbate existing environmental problems, they may occur in shorter timescales then we would prefer, and they will in many instances overwhelm our capacity to react sufficiently.

It is by now familiar to hear the sentiment that those who are least responsible for this problem are those who find themselves now most exposed to it. Societies that are least developed will suffer the most. Perversely, in a climate changing world people living subsistence livelihoods may prove more resilient than we think, at least in a political sense. If one's daily existence is a life and death struggle it will simply be more of the same, and finding someone to blame may be the least of your worries. But for people in developed countries a comparatively small change could be felt much harder. Imagine for example the necessity of regularly having to walk 100 metres to a water bowser for one's daily fresh water. In a developed country this may seem a great imposition on Mondeo Man especially if he's run out of petrol, but to someone in Sub-Saharan Africa it would be a great luxury. Our mental preparedness for such possibilities is very low, the African could take them in her mental stride (and it is of course usually women who collect water). The mere fact that people in northern latitudes believe they are therefore less susceptible to climate change might actually make them feel more vulnerable should even modest negative impacts occur. In other words, a great and painful adjustment may be called for in developed countries, and although people in such countries will have greater physical resources at their disposal, it remains to be seen how their mental and political preparedness will bear up.

Our most imponderable mental blockage is simply not knowing when – and what - is going to happen. Doug Randall, commenting on a paper he along with Peter Schwartz had been commissioned by the Pentagon to write on the implications of climate change for the security of the United States said simply "We don't know where we are in the process. It could start tomorrow and we would not know for another five years."[20] 'It' being what? In their paper, Randall and Schwartz looked at the possibility of the North Atlantic Meridonial Overturning Current (MOC) being reduced – this being the current which brings huge quantities of warm water from the southern hemisphere north and takes cold water south. Popularly known as the Gulf Stream, this keeps some of North America and a good part of north west Europe warmer than it otherwise would be. In the case of the UK, this temperature differential is around 5°C above 'normal.' The 2004 film The Day After Tomorrow provided a Hollywood-hokum vision of how abrupt could be the impacts of the reduction or total collapse of the MOC. The reality is rather different and less alarming, but should not lead to complacency. Randall and Schwartz recall the '8,200 year event,' when there was a sudden (in paleological terms) change which led to a near collapse of the MOC and which resulted in a near 6°C cooling. The 8,200 year event was brought about by a general warming of the climate which led to melting of the North American Laurentide ice sheet, and the consequent flow of two glacial lakes, Agassiz and Ojibway, into the North Atlantic. The impact of less dense, fresh cold water on the northern flow of the MOC meant that its warming effect was reduced, and a cool period of 150 years resulted, at least over those parts of the northern hemisphere most reliant on the MOC.[21]

A simplistic (and therefore easier to sell) picture of the future may appear to show that whilst the UK will be part of a world where average temperatures rise, we will be 'protected' by a balancing reduction of the warming effect of the MOC. Such a fine balance is probably unlikely to be struck, although it would be rather ironic if Britain were covered in an ice sheet whilst the south of Europe baked in perennial heatwaves. We may not have to quaff English wine after all. But our weather could still look very different to what it is now. In their scenario (not prediction) Randall and Schwartz suggest on the basis of an early big drop in MOC:

Each of the years from 2010-2020 see average temperature drops throughout Northern Europe, leading to as much as a

6 degree Fahrenheit drop in ten years. Average annual rainfall in this region decrease by nearly 30%; and winds are up to 15% stronger on average. The climatic conditions are more severe in the continental interior regions of Asia and North America. The effects of the drought are more devastating than the unpleasantness of the temperature decreases in the agricultural and populated areas. With the persistent reduction of precipitation in these areas, lakes dry-up, river flow decreases, and fresh water supply is squeezed, overwhelming available conservation options and depleting fresh water reserves. The Mega-droughts begin in key regions in Southern China and Northern Europe and around 2010 and last throughout the full decade. At the same time, areas that were relatively dry over the past few decades receive persistent years of torrential downfall, flooding rivers, and regions that traditionally relied on dryland agriculture.[22]

Let's remember that this is but a scenario and not a prediction – but it is based on a scientific understanding of the possible impacts of MOC failure. What it does is to warn us that climate change is not a simple progression, which will necessarily follow a simple pathway. We should be focused on the possibility of a very turbulent pathway – which is bound to have turbulent socio-economic consequences. This view certainly became mainstream in the Pentagon, if not within the Bush administration itself. The U.S. Army chief of staff, Gen. George Casey told a Washington audience in 2007 that 'the world will soon face an era of persistent conflict or drawn-out confrontations between state, non-state and individual actors fuelled by the impacts of globalisation, competition for energy, demographic trends, climate change, proliferation of weapons of mass destruction and failed or failing states that can provide safe havens for terrorists.'[23] What General Casey didn't say, or wasn't reported saying, was that of all the causes of conflict he cited climate change is likely to be the only threat multiplier which could make all the others worse. The UK government recognised this when it chose to use its chairmanship of the UN Security Council in spring, 2007 to devote a session to the security implications of climate change.

The three main sources of conflict likely to be exacerbated by climate change are food, energy and water. Perhaps a new acronym, FEW, may one day come to represent this triad of pressurised resources. Food and energy are somewhat different to water, since water is not yet a significant traded commodity if one excludes bottled water, which by volume is neither here nor there, nor even shipped in bulk, although that may change. Barcelona now buys imported water delivered by tanker from abroad. Food and energy, being heavily traded in globalised markets will suffer first in any downturn and are closely interlinked, food being highly dependent on energy, mainly oil, for transportation. The 'just in time' model on which food is bought and sold relies on steady and dependable supply chains in order to work. Any disruption, however slight is more likely to interrupt the supply chain than if stocks of food were stored at strategic points. This approach was partly determined by the desire to prevent finance being tied up in warehouses, partly by the desire for fresher products from more far-flung locations and also – consequent on the latter – changing tastes in food which have lead to more varied diets in developed countries. A further consequence of this last aspect is the growing demand for protein and water wasteful meat production, as more people in developing countries can afford to eat meat. The World Bank estimates that meat production will have to rise by 80 per cent by 2030 to meet demand, and cereals will have to rise by 50 per cent.[24]

The liberalisation of trade means that more protein is eaten in countries in which it is not produced. British government agricultural policy recognises this but firmly reinforces the view that it is not the government's role to determine whether the UK should be self sufficient, or even have a hand at all in deciding whether x-amount of any food variety should be derived from domestic sources. Food policy is a free market issue, as Gordon Brown said "Attempting to pursue national food security in isolation from the global context is unlikely to be practicable, sustainable or financially rational"[25] All this appears fine when the system works properly (which it doesn't, since in the developing world 40 per cent of food is wasted in storage and distribution,[26] but it doesn't take much to upset the equilibrium. A rumour – or even a recommendation for a recipe ingredient on the Delia Smith show - can disrupt the carefully calibrated supply chain. If the cause of the shortage is more serious, and occurs in a way in which the government is perceived to exercise little power (e.g. by having no intervention stocks of its own) then panic buying is likely to follow. Perhaps less so than with the supply of petrol and diesel, the shadow of panic buying nevertheless falls over any commodity when consumers believe that the only protection they may have against a shortage is to stock up as fast as possible themselves. This after all is a natural market response.

The first noticeably pervasive and deleterious effect climate change will have may well be its impacts on the supply chains of various foodstuffs long before the UK or other developed countries themselves are directly impacted by any persistent changes in climate. The greater frequency of extreme weather events – a failed or even mistimed monsoon; deepening drought, be it in Africa, China, Australia or the American Mid-West; or conditions which enhance the spread of pests: all threaten food supply, even if there may be some short term gains in some crop growing areas because of a warmer climate. The pressures for increased food production (never mind just stabilising existing levels in more hostile conditions), and not least if we are serious about achieving the Millennium Development Goal (MDG) of eradicating hunger by 2015, brings the challenge into a stark realisation that the carrying capacity of the globe is at breaking point already, never mind the additional problem of climate change, or the endemic inefficiency of the systems we use to distribute food. Consider the use of water in food production – if we are to achieve the MDG objective on hunger, we will need to double the amount of water we use for irrigation by 2050. Given that only 11% of available fresh water, from river flow and groundwater sources is available to us, the gravity of the situation is undeniable.[27] Prof. Lester Brown, of the Earth Policy Institute has made this point over and over again in his series of books titled Plan B. He notes that in many developing countries, but especially in India and China, groundwater sources have been significantly diminished, and boreholes are having to be sunk ever deeper to tap what reserves are left – reserves which have taken centuries to develop. Indeed, in some Chinese cities, groundwater levels have sunk so low that building developments have been curtailed – the foundations of existing buildings having fallen prey to subsidence.[28]

For those who can afford to pay higher prices for food, none of this need worry them too much, at least in the immediate future, and if there are occasional shortages of some products

– perhaps green beans from Kenya – then so be it. Our diets can change, and it is unlikely that we will have to return to food rationing – that of course would be a repudiation of all the benefits free trade policies promise. But a switch to some level of protectionism in food supply seems likely in the medium term. Developing countries with fast growing populations will have to choose between cash crops for export or staple crops for home consumption. The latter will prove to be the most efficient way of feeding hungry mouths, but will inevitably lead to political tensions within the world trade system, which is creaking along as never before (the 2008 U.S. presidential candidates have illustrated with this their alternating passions for protecting U.S. jobs and dishing out the mantra of global wealth creation). There is already evidence that producing countries are tightening the flow of exports. The Times reported in April 2008 that "key rice producers banned exports of rice to ensure that their own people could continue to afford to buy the staple: India, China, Vietnam and Egypt have all blocked exports."[29] In Britain it was reported that "rice is being rationed by shopkeepers in Asian neighbourhoods to prevent hoarding. Tilda, the biggest importer of basmati rice, said that its buyers – who sell to the curry and Chinese restaurant trade as well as to families – were restricting customers to two bags per person" whilst in the US "Wal-Mart have rationed rice sales to protect dwindling supplies."[30]

Agricultural subsidies for farmers in the developed world provide a continuing platform for protectionist debates, and the failure of the so-called Doha Development Round of the World Trade Organisation talks demonstrates how entrenched protectionism is. And this is true in a world which has yet to feel that much strain brought about by climate change. Defence analyst C. J. Dick, writing on the future sources of conflict, said:

Agarian societies with explosive population growth will find croplands being exhausted. This will force migration to cities where such economic refugees from the land will overwhelm inadequate infrastructures and suffer also from under- or unemployment. This in turn will often lead to rising crime and political instability which can destroy governments and create failed states and humanitarian crises.[31]

Food riots have already taken place, most notably in Mexico (the so-called 'tortilla riots') and whilst these may have been influenced by the rising cost of flour as a result of more land being turned over to 'food for fuel' crops, it would seem premature to write off the prospect of future discontent purely based on the transition from crop to another. It is conceivable at least that a government could step in and say that it was insisting on food crops being grown to feed hungry mouths rather than slake thirsty gas guzzlers. Conceivable, anyway. But the wipe-out of a year's harvest by some climate change related weather event or trend is beyond the power of any government to reverse. In such an event, resorting to a begging bowl amongst the international community will be the default option, and if the international community is itself distracted, then we shall see the victims being left to their own devices, a not unfamiliar phenomenon today even when the level of international aid and our capacity to deliver it is often spoken of as if it barely needed improvement.

Looking more closely at water as a source of future resource conflicts, Dick posited that by 2015-20, "over 3 billion people in 48 states are likely to be living in water-stressed countries. Most of them will be in Africa, the Middle East, South Asia and North East Asia, with the Middle East and North Africa faring worst." Al Gore, in his film An Inconvenient Truth talked of Himalayan glacial meltwaters feeding the fresh water needs of 40% of the world's population, a source of water which climate change will temporarily increase through more rapid melting, before it falls into long term decline. In this region, two countries with historical enmities towards each other, both members of the nuclear-armed club (outside the Non-Nuclear Proliferation Treaty), India and Pakistan may be forced into greater competition for water. Between India and Bangladesh – the latter a country most often cited as being the world's largest country susceptible to flooding through sea level rise – 30 million refugees may have to seek shelter elsewhere on a permanent basis. It seems unlikely that Bangladesh could cope internally with such a shift in population. India is already building a wall along its border with Bangladesh.

Another wall, now completed, has been built between Israel and the Palestinian territories. It has been said that part of the raison d'etre for the course of this wall has been to place Palestinian wells on the Israeli side. Regardless of the truth of that, the Middle East is possibly one of the most water stressed regions on the planet. Dick notes that "Seventeen water basins have great potential for disputes within the next 10 years, with relatively immediate problems existing between Turkey on one hand and Iraq and Syria on the other; between Egypt, Ethiopia and Sudan; between Israel, Jordan, Syria and Lebanon; and between Kyrgyzstan, Uzbekistan and Kazakhstan." Some of these countries are already, or have recently been engaged in conflict and concerns for the future avoidance of conflict will not be lessened by the knowledge that amongst their number the active pursuit of nuclear power is underway, or that some of them may hold the key to our future energy supplies.

Climate change as a threat multiplier will exacerbate known enmities, with water and food key motivators. Most predictions of its impacts show the Mediterranean region suffering much more drought. Where might Egypt get the extra water to keep us in new potatoes, if not from the Nile? What if Sudan wants the same dwindling water? The export of Israeli citrus fruit could similarly dry up. The only way for some countries to preserve their export markets will be to take more of their neighbours' water.

Energy demand, just from coal, oil and gas is predicted to rise globally from around nine billion tonnes of oil equivalent (t.o.e.) today to 14 billion toe by 2030 according to the International Energy Agency. Much of this growth will be in Asia and the growing economies. Much of it will be supplied by countries most prone to instability. There is no doubt that most of the global political elite now understand that a continued reliance on fossil fuels spells climate change disaster – but feel largely helpless, knowing too that without at least maintaining current levels of fossil fuel consumption, our economies would grind to a halt. The coincidental supply and demand high-wire act experienced in 2008 merely compounds the problem. It should not be automatically taken as read that high prices for fossil fuels will necessarily help the fight against climate change. In one respect it will – higher fossil fuel prices make renewable energy sources more competitive. But it should be noted that before investors take that proposition into account when making decisions about investing in long term developments (which may also require a high R & D commitment) they would want to be sure that fossil fuel prices were likely to remain high. That much is not certain – predicting the price of oil in a few years' time has never been easy, indeed it may be thought a mug's game. Some are willing to take a stab at it, and in doing so one analyst at least illustrated possibly another beneficial aspect of high fossil fuel prices, at least so far as climate change is concerned. Albert Edwards, of the Société Général in June 2008 predicted oil prices would fall from their then peak of $142 a barrel to just $60 a barrel. His analysis of why this would be so was predicated on the probability of a global recession having reduced demand for oil. A reduction in the demand for oil of course would lead to a reduction in carbon emissions too.[32] The follow-on question then becomes whether in a recession there would be sufficient interest in investing in alternative energy – given that in these circumstances the earlier incentive for doing so would have greatly diminished. The only approach that could possibly square these contradictory pressures is massive government intervention, a subject we shall return to.

Whilst the route to a low or zero carbon based economy is therefore unclear, our reliance on fossil fuels is only marginally impacted by high prices. High prices have led to switching between fossil fuels – the UK 'dash for gas' is a good example of that, when cheaper gas replaced expensive coal (a purely accidental consequence of which was a reduction in carbon dioxide emissions, enabling the UK to claim it was on course to meet the Kyoto carbon reduction targets). High prices may lead to moderate decreases in net fossil fuel usage, but also encourage investment in more far flung and difficult resources. In this context we have seen the oil majors, buoyed by historically high profits, abandoning their 'green' commitments of the late 1990s and early 2000s and rushing to exploit the new 'black gold rush' in the tar sands of Alberta, which now permits Canada to claim to hold the world's second largest oil reserves after Saudi Arabia. Shell notably pulled out of its investment in the London Array – the UK's largest proposed wind farm in the Thames estuary – so as to concentrate more on its core business, which is oil not energy per se. One can understand the oil majors' dilemma – with the rise of Arab nationalism, and other governments (e.g. Venuzuela) wanting to derive better value from their reserves, what's left of the 'Seven Sisters' hold a much reduced share of proven oil reserves. They need new reserves to maintain their shareholders' confidence. Hence, the greater access to polar waters afforded by melting ice opens up a whole new range of possibilities.

This detour around oil supply issues leads to an obvious conclusion: whilst high prices may lead to greater efficiencies in the way that oil is used, the net growth in demand will continue unabated, and the most we can wish for is that instead of doing 35 mph to the gallon, our cars will do 60 mph. This does not mean that we will abate the amount of driving done – that looks set to increase, and has increased without remission since cars were first mass produced. Road transport is the UK's fastest growing source of carbon dioxide emissions, alongside aviation which is essentially the same thing in market terms. This may change if there is a prolonged period of decline in personal income. But the evidence of previous oil shocks shows that provided personal income growth outpaces fuel inflation, then there is no incentive to seek a more efficient vehicle. Indeed, the response to the 1970s oil shock was to encourage designers to create more efficient engines which, when the price pressure disappeared, could simply be made larger, running on less fuel than equivalent engine capacity sizes before the shock. Once again, only government intervention can correct this trend if we are to secure carbon abatement objectives.

Much of the previous discussion considered well known themes and there is an abundance of evidence to show us what happened during previous oil shocks. Some of those 'shocks' let's not forget were manufactured not by natural circumstances but by cartels – either OPEC or the oil majors – openly and secretly at different times simply to boost their incomes. What if there were to be an energy shock brought about by climate change? The UK government Department of Business, Enterprise and Regulatory Reform (BERR – formerly known as the Department of Trade and Industry) runs a group of blue skies thinkers known as the Foresight programme. One of their scenarios – known as Tribal Trading - for the mid twenty first century runs thus:

> The world has been through a sharp and savage energy shock. The global economic system is severely damaged and infrastructure is falling into disrepair. Long-distance travel is a luxury that few can afford and for most people, the world has shrunk to their own community. Cities have declined and local food production and services have increased. There are still some cars, but local transport is typically by bike and by horse. There are local conflicts over resources: lawlessness and mistrust are high.[33]

Oil shocks manufactured by short term greed can be discounted in the system – that is, those 'in the know' anticipate that corrections in the market will eventually get us back onto an even keel and all will be well. That has been the experience – the lesson – of the past. But getting to work by bike or horse has never been part of the received wisdom, and cannot be countenanced. That could turn out to be a mistake.

What will society be like by 2050 if climate change continues unabated? The threats we have already examined may be manageable, but at what cost? This question is impossible to answer, and where attempts have been made, e.g. by seeking to define a 'social cost of carbon' there is no satisfactory conclusion. It is an issue that economists will grapple with for as long as there are two economists left in the room to debate whatever the 'discount rate' should be.[34] For those who are not economists, and who do not worry whether GDP growth by June, 2050 will be stunted because of climate change mitigation measures by three months or six months, the question is what happens to my neighbourhood, my village or town, my country? Whilst always a matter of conjecture, efforts have been made to forecast the future – we have already seen some of those above, in terms of sources of conflict, high energy prices and the actual changes in climate. In Forecasting the Future, a document produced by the Energy Savings Trust, we are presented with a (tautologically titled) "2050: a fictional vision of the future." In part this says

> Buildings might suffer if wind speeds increase, with perhaps one million properties damaged by the worst storms. Flooding is a potential problem as winter rains grow heavier and sea levels rise. Flood and sea defences will need to protect over two million houses and the 40 per cent of industry that lie near to coasts or river estuaries; that is equivalent to £200 billion of assets. In particular, investment will be needed to protect London and other key places from flooding as well as vulnerable installations such as nuclear power stations, even after they have closed down. Within 50 years from now, significant pats of East Anglia will have to be heavily defended against rising seas, including ports like Felixtowe. Some land could be returned to the sea, called managed

retreat, as has already happened at Paull Home Strays. Home insurance could go through the roof, or perhaps be withdrawn altogether in some places, with annual insurance claims reaching the £800 million mark . . There are mixed blessings for public health . . summer heatwaves could see an increase in heat related deaths. The heat will also require more careful food handling to avoid rises in food poisoning. Without action to make transport infrastructure more climate robust, it could grind to a halt as rails buckle and foundations subside in hot summer while rain and flooding lead to landslides . . [35]

This all sounds eerily familiar – parts of this 'fictional future' had already occurred by 2008 – just not quite on the scale required to move us very much. A bleaker picture, and it once again comes with a health warning because it is only a scenario, was produced by the Foresight team, based in the Office of Science and Technology and chaired by Prof. Sir David King, the government's former chief scientist. Here we are again, looking at the year 2055 in the 'Tribal Trading' scenario, which is chillingly described as 'a rather moderate version of a conceivably darker and more dystopic nightmare that extends some current trends.' [36]

This is a vision of a 'pre-Mediaevalist' society where

There are no longer clear and well-enforced national borders. Rather there are relatively separate and self-governing city-states, a re-localisation of the world. Surrounding such walled cities there is an enormously dangerous and chaotic environment which few people will enter without arms. Long range travel is dangerous and only undertaken by those who are armed. No longer do states possess the monopoly of legitimate violence. And there are soe powerful empires, of McDonalds and Microsoft, although future empires are likely to be based on upon the control of water and energy sources which are in increasingly short supply guarded by armed gangs. With such patterns it is likely that the first shall be the last and the last shall be first. Global cities like London will have become ungovernable and unregulatabe.[37]

Far fetched? It is of course impossible to say, although it does no harm to question just how robust our present form of civilisation is when in some quarters for example, we harbour notions of a 'fortress Europe' – a fortress built to repel hordes of unwanted migrants. There are not many stepping stones between a bureaucratic prerogative and hard-edged supremacy. On the other hand, perhaps we – in the developed world – will be predisposed to offer a welcoming hand to those who are dispossessed by climate change. In humble contrition, countries like the UK which may escape the worst impacts of climate change, but which are its historic culprits will open our shores to hundreds of thousands, perhaps millions of environmental refugees, a lifeboat of sorts. It is very hard to envisage. Alternatively, in a scenario painted by James Lovelock in the The Revenge of Gaia, "Despite all our efforts to retreat sustainably, we may be unable to prevent a global decline into a chaotic world ruled by brutal warlords on a devastated Earth. If this happens we should think of those small groups of monks in mountain fastnesses like Montserrat or on islands like Iona and Lindisfarne who served this vital purpose," that purpose being to guard the best of what we were.[38]

The question of where we are on this road to 'war' has still not been resolved, since it is clearly as difficult to chart if not more so then was the road to war in the 1930s. Our difficulty is compounded by the knowledge that whatever happens, whatever form this 'war' takes, it will not be over in a few years and there will in that time be an abundance of contrary evidence played for all it is worth by climate change detractors who will always have a ready audience. In this regard, this assessment of Churchill's perseverance is heartwarming to anyone engaged in political campaigning:

> Churchill was far more receptive to alarming intelligence (among other reasons because of his interest in proving that government policies were all wrong) than were the various governments and prime ministers who were preoccupied with their day to day responsibilities and wanted to prove the success of their own policies." [39]

Always proving the success of their own policies is the original sine qua non of politicians, it is the condition which ensures that apologies for the gravest of errors more often than not commence with the words 'If I have appeared to make a complete bollocks of things . . .

Notes

1. Winston Churchill, *The Gathering Storm*, Reprint Society, London, 1948, xi

2. *ibid*, p.50

3. *Times*, 29th March 2006

4. A month after Rowan Williams's 'genocide' comments, the Bishop of London, Richard Chartres turned the screw a little bit more with a bit of advice – it is sinful to fly. He said "Making selfish choices such as flying on holiday or buying a large car are a symptom of sin. Sin is not just a restricted list of moral mistakes. It is living a life turned in on itself where people ignore the consequences of their actions." *Sunday Times*, 23rd July 2006. More recently another bishop, Gordon Mursell, the Bishop of Stafford was hauled over the coals for, in the ways that things are reported, describing civilised people like you and me as child abusers. He said in his diocese magazine "Josef Fritzl [the recently arrested Austrian child abuser]

represents merely the most extreme form of a very common philosophy of life. I will do what makes me happy and if that causes others to suffer, hard luck. In fact, you could argue that, by our refusal to face the truth about climate change we are as guilty as he is - we are in effect locking our children and grandchildren into a world with no future and throwing away the key." *Birmingham Mail*, 4th June 2008. The fact that Mursell perhaps inadvisedly coupled his comment with a reference to Fritzl merely allowed the media to extract an apology from him, without addressing the substance of what he had said, or really implied.

5. Speech to All Party Parliamentary Climate Change Group, Westminster, February, 2006

6. Clive Ponting, *1940 Myth and Reality* Hamish Hamilton, London, 1990 p141

7. *Hansard*, 9th June 2008 : Column 103. Ann Widdecombe may have spoken for a significant silent minority when she told me: "I was one of three MPs who opposed the Climate Change Bill because I believe the whole thing has now reached a degree of disproportionality that was completely unnecessary. Britain creates 2% of the world's carbon emissions and yet we are taking a huge unilateral action which is likely to leave us uncompetitive and to make no one iota of difference to the temperature of the planet . . the only amendments I shall be signing are those which make things easier, not harder." (Letter to author dated 10th July 2008)

8. Hermann Scheer, *Energy Autonomy: The economic, social and technological case for renewable energy*, Earthscan, London 2007

9. Joseph Stiglitz and Linda Bilmes, The Three Trillion Dollar War: The true cost of the Iraq conflict, Allen Lane, London 2008

10. The current round of negotiations held under the auspices of the UNFCCC are actually structured around upgrading the existing Kyoto Protocol, not replacing it with a brand new framework.

11. Carbon sink failures occur when the natural ability of an eco-system, such as the world's oceans or its tropical rainforests can no longer absorb CO_2 and may actually start releasing previously absorbed CO_2 making a net contribution to GHG concentrations in the atmosphere; positive feedbacks, as well as the foregoing may occur when e.g. ice melts and reduces the reflectivity of the surface – thus absorbing more radiation from the sun, if the exposed surface below is water, as is the case with the Polar ice cap; or, it could be caused by the melting of permafrost releasing long stored methane, a far more potent greenhouse gas than CO_2.

12. *Sunday Times* 10th February 2008

13. See the National Coalition Against Censorship website for a comprehensive examination of government interference; also the *Guardian* 10th July 2008 – it was not just the science that was being suppressed, but sensible policies to deal with it, thus Vice President Dick Cheney sought to delete "any discussion of the human health consequences of climate change"

14. *New York Times* 21st April 2002

15. The full memo can be viewed at www.nrdc.org/media/docs/020403.pdf - page one of the memo is reproduced at Annex Two

16. *Guardian*, 24th June 2008

17. *Climate Change Controversies: a simple guide*, Royal Society, London, June 2007

18. see text and figure 28.5 in Schellnhuber et al, *Avoiding Dangerous Climate Change*, Cambridge, 2006, p270

19. www.columbia.edu/~jeh1/2008/TwentyYearsLater_20080623.pdf

20. *Observer*, 22nd February 2004

21. Peter Schwartz and Doug Randall, *An Abrupt Climate Change Scenario and Its Implications for United States National Security*, October 2003; the UK's Natural Environment Research Council is leading research into the MOC with its Rapid Climate Change Programme. NERC is developing regular monitoring of the MOC after a study reported in Nature in 2005 claimed that between 1957 and 2001 there may have been a reduction of the MOC by 30%

22. *ibid*

23. Army prepares for Future of Conflict, Casey says, American Forces Press Services, 14.8.07 at www.defenselink.mil/news

24. (Defra press release "Government sets out 21st century challenges for food in the UK" 7th July 2008)

25. *ibid*

26. *ibid*
27. see *Global Environment Outlook, GEO4: environment for development*, United Nations Environment Programme, 2007
28. Lester R. Brown, *Plan B2.0: Rescuing a Planet Under Stress and a Civilisation in Trouble*, Norton, New York, 2006
29. *Times*, 24th April 2008
30. *ibid*
31. C. J. Dick, *The Future of Conflict: Looking out to 2020*, Defence Academy of the United Kingdom, Camberley, Surrey, April 2003
32. *Sunday Times*, 29th June 2008
33. http://www.foresight.gov.uk/search/index.php?searchTerm=tribal+trading&searchSubmit=GO
34. Simply put the discount rate is the value one gives to future economic activity, thus £100 today may be worth £75 in ten year's time; but it is always assumed that people in the future will be richer, since their GDP will be greater. Naturally, it gets more complicated than that.
35. *Forecasting the Future: Changing climate, changing behaviour*, Energy Savings Trust, October 2004
36. *Intelligent Infrastructure Futures, Scenarios Toward 2055 – Perspective and Process*, Office of Science and Technology, DTI, London 2005
37. *ibid*
38. James Lovelock, *The Revenge of Gaia*, Penguin, London 2007, p 198
39. Michael Handel, *War, Strategy and Intelligence*, Routledge, London 1989 p 191

2

our promise to you:
last in, first out

I believe the difficulties with the current climate debate is the trouble with so much international politics: a reluctance to face up to reality and the practical action needed to tackle problems.

Prime Minister Tony Blair [1]

'The trouble with so much international politics' boils down to one thing: international politics has never developed its own enforcer. There are no police, no courts and no sanctions to enforce a punishment for collective failure, as opposed to the failure of an individual state (and preferably a weak one at that). The UN can only succeed with an encompassing collective goal where it secures universal consent and compliance. Where there are failures, the only power at the Secretary-General's disposal seems to be the power to name and shame – and since the shamed are often the UN's most powerful members it is a double edged sword. Thus, the wholesale inability of the Kyoto Protocol's Annex One countries – the developed world countries – to meet their Kyoto GHG reduction targets has led to little more than oft repeated re-affirmations to do better 'next time.' Self-indulgent annual hand wringing sessions have become the norm, their impotence masked by the occasional success – which may have been nothing more than a commitment to carry on talking. This stumbling progress may not be entirely due to a reluctance to do anything substantial; it can also be the consequence of confusion and an institutionalised culture of unhurried diplomacy. The sheer complexity of the UNFCCC COP/MOP process does not help. The differing economic demands of countries are deeply woven into their diplomatic expectations. Long standing commitments to sustainable development where perhaps the goals should seem somewhat simpler to achieve are undermined by the record of the UN members which has not inspired confidence. There is a contest too between climate change mitigation efforts and climate change adaptation efforts. Not surprisingly then that at the 'African COP,' held in Nairobi in 2006, the main outcome was the Nairobi work plan on adaptation: those countries which face the worst consequences of climate change in the very near future want to see immediate action to help them cope with it. It would not be much use telling somebody flooded out of their home that a wind turbine might help avert the situation getting worse in the future. The Nairobi COP perhaps also showed that there exists a deep distrust amongst developing countries of the promises from the Annex One countries to reduce their GHG emissions. All the more reason to fund adaptation projects sooner rather than later. Added to this distrust is the long history of the developed countries' failure to honour their other long-standing commitments, delivered with all the hyperbolic razzamatazz we have come to expect from exclusive, elite circuses such as the G8.

Prominent amongst these grand global promises can be cited the 1970 commitment of developed countries to devote 0.7% of their GDP to overseas development aid (ODA). Whilst the 0.7% figure was pretty arbitrary it nevertheless set a realisable goal.[2] But by 2008, only five countries had achieved it: Denmark, Norway, Netherlands, Luxembourg and Sweden. Indeed, according to UNICEF UK, "despite rich countries having never been richer, just 0.25 per cent of the GNI (approximately $68 billion) is given in development assistance; around half of what it was in 1960."[3] Despite some countries' efforts, a report from the OECD prior to the 2008 G8 meetings in Japan "showed total development aid among the world's 22 major aid donors fell 8.4 per cent in real terms in 2007."[4] The Japanese Foreign Minister, Masahiko Komura said "Each G8 country is determined to strengthen development aid." The evidence necessarily reinforces the view that such G8 pledges cannot be taken at face value.

Then there were the Millennium Development Goals, agreed at the UN Millennium Summit in 2000. These promised to eradicate extreme poverty and hunger, achieve universal primary education, promote gender equality and empower women, reduce child mortality, improve maternal health, combat HIV/AIDS and other diseases, ensure environmental sustainability and develop a global partnership for development – all by 2015. But once again, despite some successes the overwhelming picture is one of efforts meandering off course, with an EU report saying that even the EU's commitment as the world's largest donor was tapering off with its ratio of ODA to GNI falling from 0.41 per cent in 2006 to 0.38 per cent in 2007 – a pattern reflected in UK aid flows.[5]

There has been progress towards fulfilling the MDG pledges, but it is unlikely that many of them will be delivered by 2015, and given current economic and climate change trends we shouldn't be surprised if there are reversals, e.g. in reducing the incidence of malaria.[6] But whether or not the MDGs are realised by 2015 is not entirely down to development aid. Pro-trade liberalisation politicians and economists argue that the removal of trade barriers invigorates local economies, and this, a variant of Ronald Reagan's vision of 'trickle down' economics will do the trick. All this trickling down will apparently contribute to a rising tide 'which will lift all boats.' It is astonishing to note the extent to which this crude theory has been adopted even by left-of-centre governments, including our own since the evidence points to a growing worldwide poverty gap, but that is not a question for now: the real question is to what extent Reaganonomics, so closely identified with the 'success' of the world economy since the fall of the Berlin Wall in 1990, makes it easier or harder to tackle climate change and to what extent global trade liberalisation is compatible with promises to find a solution to climate change. Very often, those who question trade liberalisation will be warned that since problems with the environment are global, they need a global solution and therefore that solution can only happen by building on the form of globalisation which contributed so much to the problem in the first place. We only seem to know one form of globalisation, after all. It is a form of elliptic reasoning designed to conflate the use of two different and largely incompatible concepts.

One amongst many good examples of how globalised commerce can trump conservation is provided by The Film and Bag Federation (FBF) of the United States, a 'business unit of the Society of the Plastic Industry, Inc.' It had heard that some countries had got it into their heads that plastic bags could cause an environmental problem and were even contemplating banning them. Many people were becoming familiar with the Republic of Ireland's plastic bag tax, which costs shoppers around 10p for every new bag they use. The Irish tax was introduced to combat litter and many people, not least consumers themselves welcomed the tax. Vast reductions have been made in the amount of plastic blowing around the streets and country lanes of the Republic. But many countries have had to face up to this most ephemeral yet persistent of problems.

In Bangladesh polythene bags were banned in March 2002 "after they were found to have been one of the key causes of the 1998 floods which led to the inundation of approximately two-thirds of the country. It was discovered that discarded plastic bags were choking the drainage system"[7] In Bombay, plastic bags were banned after they were found to be blocking the sewerage system. Police raids have taken place on shops and factories that handle or manufacture plastic bags. In Taiwan steps have been taken to reduce the distribution of free plastic bags to cut pollution.

These actions reflect growing concerns with our throwaway society and the serious consequences our thoughtless behaviour can have on the environment. Governments and local authorities should be able to react to these concerns and take appropriate action. But not if it interferes with trade liberalisation, it seems. The FBF sent a delegation to the US Department of Commerce to "discuss FBF's concerns about recent trading partner actions to ban or tax plastic bags. Commerce Department representatives from numerous departments met with [them] to discuss policies in South Africa, Taiwan, Philippines, Bangladesh, India and Ireland . . to look into actions or proposed laws that may harm the ability of US manufacturers to conduct business in those countries. The Commerce Department will continue to monitor those countries' compliance with international trading rules."[8] This can be clearly read as a warning to any other state that considers it has an environmental problem with plastic bags to steer clear – the mighty US Department of Commerce will be watching you. And what could be the result? A referral to the World Trade Organisation's (WTO) Disputes Panel, which meets in secret and can hand down hard fines to the offending country's taxpayers. But it doesn't have to go that far. "In November 2001, the South African cabinet prohibited the distribution of thin plastic grocery bags . . which was due to be effective from January 2003. However, in the face of fierce resistance from the packaging and retail industries, the government has hinted it may relax this regulation."[9] Thus, despite the fact that a ban or tax on plastic bags would obviously apply to all bags, be they manufactured domestically or in the US, the threat of action by industry can have a chilling effect even though WTO rules (Article III) were intended only to prevent taxes being used to disadvantage imports.

But the threat of a WTO dispute can be used to force exports too. In evidence to the Environmental Audit Committee, Tom Crompton of WWF said

> "We are seeing . . the EU pushing a dispute through the WTO about re-treaded tyres in Brazil. The Brazilians are saying that they do not want any more re-treaded tyres; they have enough re-treaded tyres domestically. They do not see why they should be importing European re-treaded tyres, which are stockpiled, which will cause environmental problems in the course of their destruction, which will have all sorts of problems in terms of stagnant water which sits around them. The Brazilians are mounting a defence against the demand from the EU that they

should be able to export European re-treaded tyres to Brazil on European grounds."[10]

The expression that 'trade always trumps conservation' has a clear application here. No doubt the WTO (and the EU) could argue with Brazil that Brazilian re-treaded tyres might easily be exported, thus ensuring that any imports could be counterbalanced by exports. But what's the point? One of the greatest contributors to climate change that the growth in trade is making is in transport-related GHG emissions – and both aviation and maritime GHG emissions are exempt from the Kyoto Protocol and the grounds that they were too complicated to deal with. In the case of aviation's emissions, one might hope that the UN's International Civil Aviation Organisation (ICAO) might have dealt with them, but they have been talking without conclusion since recommendations were put forward at the ICAO Assembly in 2001. It is far easier it seems to negotiate 'open skies' agreements to liberalise aviation markets then it is to set down rigorous standards on GHG emissions.

Ironically, the EU, through its own Environment Impact Assessment of the WTO's Doha 'development round' negotiations concluded

Global environmental impacts are expected to be negative as the volume of international trade increases. The impacts on climate change and global biodiversity are adverse overall, arising primarily through increased transport and pressures for increased agricultural production in biologically sensitive areas. Local affect occur for water, air and soil quality, water quantity, soil erosion and biodiversity, and are particularly significant in areas of high existing stress. These adverse environmental

effects can in principle be countered by technology or
regulatory measures. However, in many developing countries,
environmental regulation tends to be insufficiently strong to
counter adverse effects.[11]

So a ban on plastic bags in a developing country with
weaker environmental regulations seems a ripe candidate for
pressurising with the WTO big stick – and if countries have
weak environmental regulations, how strong will they be
defending themselves in the WTO's disputes panel process?
The benefits of globalisation are meant to accrue to poorer
countries but their place is to know their place. Even the
benefits appear to have been overstated in any case. Analysis
by the New Economic Foundation show that "Between 1990
and 2001, for every $100 worth of growth in the world's
income per person, just $0.60 found its target and contributed
to reducing poverty below the $1-a-day line. To achieve
every single $1 of poverty reduction therefore requires $166
of additional global production . ."[12] In other words, the vast
majority of the benefit accrues to the developed world, but
this will come as no surprise.

The impacts of the unquestioning faith in markets, their
growth and liberalisation have been stated by Nicholas Stern
– climate change was, he said the 'greatest market failure of
all time.' GDP and GHG emissions have for decades marched
inexorably upwards in perfect lockstep, and it has yet to sink
in at the upper reaches of the political discourse that this is so.
Hence, what allegedly offers salvation for the poor will also, as
we in the rich world are generously prepared to admit, hit them
hardest too, first. It seems the pursuit of GDP growth has a
golden rule: last in, first out.

Clearly we need an investment strategy which tells us what we need to do if we want to solve the problem faster than we are creating it, rather than pinning our hopes on the partial validity of arguments about how markets deliver resource efficiencies, green technolgical advances and least cost solutions. There is some truth in all of those arguments, but their application is insufficiently directed to lend urgency to the situation. Indeed, there is a view that somehow markets are a cost-free option, since some great 'invisible hand' will dip into some equally invisible pockets to pay for the transformations required.

The Stern report, despite the many disputes which have circled round it since it was published in October, 2006 at least shines a light on what a strategy (successful or not) may cost. At the Review's high powered launch with the Prime Minister Tony Blair, Chancellor Gordon Brown and Environment Secretary David Miliband sharing the platform, Sir Nick Stern presented the outcome of his climate change inquiry. One of the conclusions of this was that we would have to spend a little extra now to avoid a lot of damage later – and this has become the mantra of successive politicians ever since. So two years later (a sizeable period in the rapid countdown to 2015, the year in which the IPCC says global greenhouse gas emissions must peak) we should return to the question of 'yes, so how much do think it will cost?' We need to ask if the Stern report really has kickstarted serious action to mitigate climate change or merely another round of musing. Are we devoting the necessary resources to the task, or is the report observed more in the breach than in compliance? And what, to be precise, did his figures really mean?

Let's begin with the last question - what did Stern actually say? In the summary of his conclusions we find this:

Ultimately, stabilisation - at whatever level - requires that annual emissions be brought down to more than 80% below current levels. This is a major challenge, but sustained long-term action can achieve it at costs that are low in comparison to the risks of inaction. Central estimates of the annual costs of achieving stabilisation between 500 and 550 ppmv CO_2e are around 1% of global GDP, if we start to take strong action now." (emphasis added)[13]

Given that Stern talks about taking action now, we must assume that any delay merely adds to the cumulative cost - we cannot 'bank' any savings made on earlier year's financial budgets. What we didn't spend in 2007 will have to be added to 2008's spend, and what wasn't spent in 2008 will have to spent in 2009 – and so on. We must also assume that the 1% of GDP is additional finance - it wouldn't have made sense for Stern to have referred to existing business as usual spending streams, just so that we can swap a few budget heads around to identify 1% which could be re-described as climate change specific. This is extra money, and more to the point it is about mitigation, achieving GHG atmospheric stabilisation, so money spent on adaptation should be treated independently.

Let's return to the 1%. This is the bottom end of expectations, given that it covers a stabilisation range which goes up to 550 ppmvCO_2e. But as is often the case with summaries, one has to dig deeper for the fuller picture. On page 239 of the Stern Review is this:

An estimate of resource costs suggests that the annual cost of cutting total GHG to about three quarters of current levels by 2050, consistent with a 550 ppmvCO_2e stabilisation level, will be in the range -1.0 to +3.5% of GDP, with an average estimate of approximately 1%.[14]

This is more precise as to the stabilisation level - there is no range starting at 500 ppmv here, it is about staying within 550ppmv, a much worse position. Naturally these are estimates, and different models as Stern acknowledges 'span a wide range' but nevertheless, given what we know about the (im) probability of keeping temperature increases below the UK and EU policy target of 2°C with a stabilisation level of 550ppm, the average cost of meeting the policy target is more likely to be higher than 1% of GDP. New research suggests that we should be preparing for a tougher task.[15] Anyway, let's not worry about that right now, but look to see where the 1% takes us, perhaps safe in the knowledge that whatever the figure should be, it certainly shouldn't be less than 1%. In UK terms, at the time of the publication of the Stern Review, 1% of GDP equated to around £13 billion pounds. Are we yet coming anywhere close to matching that?

Before seeking an answer, it is worth dwelling on a charge that could be made, which is that to devote time to this issue is equivalent to counting angels on a pin head. After all, we have got the core message haven't we, that it is a lot better to tackle climate change now than leave it to later? Isn't this question a little bit pedantic? Did we really expect UK plc to start spending £13 billion the day after Stern launched his report? Well, yes actually. The counter charge is that politicians from the UK to the EU to the US refer to Stern - but then don't seem to understand it. Or more likely, they wilfully use it to send a signal to show how switched on they are whilst at the same time minimising their effort. To date even 1%

is too much to ask, as we shall see. We might also recall, as Prof. Lester Brown has reminded us, how just one month after Pearl Harbour, Franklin Roosevelt addressed Congress and inaugurated an immediate transformation of the US economy to a total war economy. And talking of war, Prof. Joseph Stiglitz in his latest book shows how the US is spending $3 trillion on fighting the Iraq war; our contribution is around £18 billion.[16] What are we spending now to combat climate change? Are we taking the Stern Review seriously? The answer is admittedly hard to pin down. Expenditure on mitigating climate change is rather difficult to identify with any exactitude. We most seek out additional spending across the whole economy, not just government spending. We must ask whether we are looking at old budgets given new names; we must ask whether we are talking about gross expenditure or net expenditure - as Stern makes clear, some of the extra money spent will certainly lead to cost savings. Energy efficiency comes to mind. Are we talking about money with dual or single purposes? Money spent on tackling fuel poverty, which reduces people's fuel bills, may also be counted as money spent tackling climate change. And by a few renamings, civil servants may be able to boost their ministers' credibility - and reduce their call on a hard pressed Treasury. And what of, e.g. money spent pursuing a nuclear power policy? If we say we want nuclear power for its low carbon quality, does simply replacing old power stations now count towards mitigating climate change?

One can see how Nick Stern's 1% could be quickly mopped up without an extra penny being spent. So who is asking if it is being spent? I asked Defra Minister Phil Woolas the following rather long-winded question in a meeting of the Environmental Audit Committee:

. . if we [are to] aim for a more stringent target [don't] we have to spend more money to achieve it? He settled on one per cent of GDP and suggested we should try and stay within a target of between 500 ppm and 550 ppm and then later on in further articles he has written 450 ppm, so that is there and well-established. Obviously it would cost more to be tougher. Are we spending that one per cent now? Is that an extra one per cent of GDP or is it what was already being spent at the time that Stern published his report? Are we monitoring this money? Are we trying to achieve it? Surely the best way to try and convince others that we are serious is if we are going into negotiations and we can prove that we are doing it and we are abiding by our own report that we commissioned. If we are not meeting even one per cent, which is at the low end of expectations, then surely nobody can take us seriously.

Mr Woolas (Climate Change Minister): The point that the United Kingdom's credibility overseas in these negotiations must be matched by a credible performance domestically is of extreme importance. This is why we place so much emphasis on pointing out the United Kingdom's progress in the reduction of greenhouse gas emissions. There has been a debate in recent weeks about the UK's performance and the confusion of CO_2 and greenhouse gas emissions is more than just a semantic point; it is a very important point. The creation of the carbon budgets as required by the Climate Change Bill and the work that we are doing with the Committee - this is one of the reasons why we wanted to get it established and up and running in shadow form and we are very grateful to the House that that has been permitted - and the analysis of the expenditure, revenue and capital in that regard is clearly very important. The honest answer to your question is that at

the moment we are not able to do that as robustly as we will
be able to do. The second point is that we act in co-ordination
with the European Union. The European Union's package is a
very important part of the equation and where we can point to
specific goals. The honest answer to your question is not yet.[17]

Or more succinctly – 'I don't know.' The biggest single player
in the economy is of course the government - responsible
for expenditure worth close to £550 billion, or 41.5% of GDP
(in 2006/2007). If the government were to match Stern's 1%,
one would therefore expect it to be spending in the order of
£5.5 billion on climate change mitigation measures – its share
of GDP. For the year 2006/2007 research by the House of
Commons Library suggests that the government's actual total -
which includes money spent on fuel poverty objectives - came
to just £650 million, a shade over 10% of its share of one per
cent of GDP. If we removed the Warmfront Scheme, which was
originally designed as an anti-fuel poverty strategy, then the
figure would be halved.

The most heavily touted policy to tackle climate change
(although as it has been argued, not necessarily to make a net
reduction in carbon emissions per se) is the European Union's
Emissions Trading Scheme (EU ETS). The EU ETS began life
in 2005, and the House of Commons Environmental Audit
Committee thought it was questionable whether phase one of
the EU ETS had reduced carbon emissions at all. Putting that to
one side, a paper produced by the analytical service PointCarbon
said 1.6 billion tonnes of CO_2e were traded in 2006, worth €22.5
billion, with a prediction it would drop to €18.5 billion in 2007.
According to the CIA's website, the GDP of the EU in 2007
was $14.47 trillion or shall we say around £7.23 trillion. Thus,

making a rough and ready calculation, one per cent of EU GDP comes to £72.3 billion. So the ETS was worth roughly 0.25% of EU GDP and if that percentage could translate directly into UK terms, it would result in a cost of perhaps £3.25bn in carbon trading. The cost of the EU ETS we must assume represents a considerable fraction of industry's expenditure tackling climate change. Point Carbon estimate that around 65% of companies involved have started to abate their own emissions. And let us not forget that some companies have made windfall gains out of the ETS - money which may or may not be spent mitigating climate change.

What about our individual expenditure as consumers? This is extremely difficult to pin down. Is buying that energy saving light bulb a simple straightforward item of climate change spending? Is the whole cost of a more efficient replacement central heating boiler all to be credited to a climate change effort? A report produced by the Co-operative Bank estimated that UK consumers' 'climate change' expenditure may have amounted to £5.8bn in 2006.[18] The House of Commons Library suggests that all categories of expenditure, public and private in 2006/2007 may have come to £8.5 billion. Without strict definitions on what should count towards this total it is almost impossible to come to a conclusive figure, but it would still seem to be considerably less than one per cent. But no-one knows. This is work in progress.

Now let's move to the real nub of the problem. The one per cent figure seriously understates what we have to do now, for the simple fact is we need to maximise our efforts in the early stages of this challenge - 'more sooner' is the only motto we should obey. A steady one per cent of GDP each year to 2050 will be less use than a chocolate teapot. On the government's own figures contained in recent Budgets, our CO_2 emissions have not been going down in recent years. Our efforts indeed are reducing the carbon intensity of the economy, but because the economy keeps on growing, CO_2 emissions are extremely difficult to contain. The one per cent figure over the whole period is not therefore what we should be looking at, it should not be annualised. As we come to set carbon budgets under the new Climate Change Act we should bear in mind that fact. The carbon limits we put in place in each five-year budget period must be matched by adequate resources to achieve the budgets. As yet there is no evidence we are gearing up for this, perhaps having been lulled into a false sense of security with the Stern Review's very modest sounding one per cent. For many charged with making budgetary decisions, one per cent seems so small it can almost be squeezed out of other budget lines, or even squeezed out altogether. One per cent is after all not a great leap from zero per cent.

Would an increased commitment hurt us? Not according to Adair Turner, chair of the independent Climate Change Committee established by the government and former CBI Director-General, who said

"Even if the cost of mitigating climate change for rich developed countries was as much as five per cent of GDP, this would simply mean that measured economic prosperity would have to wait till mid-2052 to reach the level it might otherwise have reached by January 2050, a level likely to about twice current levels. Given that there is no strong correlation between GDP growth and human well-being, even this much higher cost than Stern has estimated could not be considered as a conclusive argument against action."[19]

The IMF came to a similar conclusion, noting that policies needed to cut global emissions by 60% by 2040 would reduce the global economy by a mere 2.6% of what it otherwise would have been by then.[20] Bankers, speculators and sub-prime follies can achieve a lot more than that in much shorter space of time.

By June, 2008 Nick Stern had returned to his original estimates, and like a dog digging up an old bone had discovered that more of its flesh had simply disappeared – or in this case, the upper CO_2 concentration limit. He reduced his estimate of what that should be from 550ppmv to 500ppmv, and doubled his estimate of what the cost of mitigation should be to two per cent of GDP.[21] Thus in the year 2008 the UK, according to the government's most quoted expert on these matters, UK plc should have spent £28 billion on mitigating climate change – perhaps three or four times what was actually spent on the most generous estimates we can make. Given that Dr Jim Hansen has suggested that a target of 350ppmv is the maximum permissible (a target we have already missed) even Adair Turner's talk of five per cent of GDP looks passé. And to recap, this is to ignore the necessity of 'frontloading' more effort now, rather than levelling out the process to 2050 in a seamless, linear fashion. That approach is to invite the greater of positive feedbacks and carbon sink failure. By way of comparison, £28 billion is around about what the government risked on saving Northern Rock.

But one of the real political tipping points is if – and when – expenditure on mitigation is exceeded by spending on adaptation. This may not just be domestic expenditure, but international expenditure. Those countries who suffer the impacts of climate change first will expect a good part of their adaptation costs to be met by developed countries. As these costs mount, then the tension between the developed world and developing world will not only rise, but also the tension between adaptation and mitigation. Let's bear in mind that the almost impossible figures Stern now talks of is what our own effort should be to reduce our own carbon footprint not to adapt to it. Some of this may well be transferred to other economies through carbon emissions trading, but trading does not directly reduce our own footprint, and with current UK per capita emissions at 10 tonnes, it is quite obvious that this task must be addressed if the whole proposition of tackling climate change is to be taken seriously.

So, if we hear a Prime Minister, a President or an Environment Minister talking of finding a solution to climate change, what should we infer they mean by it? Once again, there really is only one correct answer, viz: that they mean to find a solution to the problem which means we'll solve it faster than we're creating it. By definition we must reduce our greenhouse gas emissions faster than we are creating them, if we wish to stabilise the concentration of GHGs in the atmosphere at a 'safe and sustainable' level.

It was not until the Gleneagles G8 Summit in 2005 that President Bush, under pressure from Tony Blair, made any significant admission that the problem of climate change was real and the G8 statement was sufficiently unambitious it mercifully merited the President's acquiescence. What Bush had been willing to subscribe to was the notion that the United States' dependency on oil (i.e. Middle Eastern oil) had to be curtailed – he once famously and with seeming sincerity described the US as being 'addicted to oil.' In reality, the most the confluence the twin issues of security of oil supply and climate change was likely to lead to was a policy of reducing carbon emissions and/

or Middle East oil intensity per unit of GDP growth coupled with the search for alternative liquid fuels, such as ethanol, 'dirty' oil from Albertan tar sands or perhaps eventually the opening up of new Alaskan oil fields. Thus, he said U.S. policy would lead to an 18% cut in CO_2 emissions intensity per unit of GDP by 2014 – but if up until 2014 GDP had grown say by 25% or 30%, this 'green' policy was actually predicated on accepting growth in greenhouse gas emissions. The point was acknowledged by James Connaughton, the Chair of the White House Environment Council shortly before the historic Bush-Blair 'breakthrough' at Gleneagles. Connaughton said:

> In the US, [emissions] have stopped, they have stabilised. But we do expect with the rates of growth that we are seeing, that we will begin to see a slight rise again in our GHG emissions. But as we apply the next generation of technology (gasification of coal for example), if we could add a substantial new base of diesel and hybrid powered vehicles, if we can get a much larger turnover of our office buildings the efficiency upgrades, that's when we can begin to see things level off. But those are hundreds of billions if not trillions of dollars of investment that occur over a 20 to 30 year time horizon. And so we could not stop the growth and reverse [of GHG emissions] and still keep economic growth in our country. And that's one of the reasons that we could not sign up to the Kyoto Protocol: It established a target that was impossible for us to achieve. And so we further set a target that is aggressive but within rationality.[22]

The 'stabilisation' Connaughton talked about had less to do with government policy than the fact that in the early years of the 21st century, the U.S. economy had suffered a mild recession, capped with the flight of more heavy industry to China. Connaughton claimed the consequent CO_2 reduction of 0.8% as a success for Bush's vision, but then admitted it hadn't been 'projected.' Despite the fact that US GHG emissions had been rising by about 1% per year since 1990, Connuaghton 'hailed the stabilisation of greenhouse gas output as a victory for the US policy of avoiding mandatory targets.' Such an approach is not atypical, since in the UK too the 'dash for gas' in the 1990s, which reduced our use of coal in electricity generation led to a reduction in emissions and has, ever since, allowed ministers to imply that the U.K's ability to meet its Kyoto target of a 12.5% reduction in GHG emissions is a testament to the success of government intervention alone rather than changes in market conditions. The length of time it generally takes to introduce and implement policies was no disincentive for the writers of the Labour Party's Pocket Policy Guide issued in September, 2000 who advanced the claim that the government had already met "the Rio target of stabilisation of greenhouse gas emissions at 1990 levels by 2000." After only three years in power on that level of performance one would have thought it should have been possible to cut at least another 15% to 20% GHG emissions by 2008, but the UK is struggling to meet its domestic 20% target by 2020. Subsequent changes in market conditions have shown that what the markets give they can just as easily take away. When coal became cheaper to use, coal's use increased, and the significant reductions in UK GHG was stopped in its tracks then reversed. To put these market changes in their proper perspective – that is within our war metaphor – we might ask how the Battle of Britain could have been won if it had been left to market forces. But at least by 2005 it appeared as if the most sceptical government – the Bush administration - had at last moved into the realm of appeasement, if not phoney war.

Notes

1. *Observer*, 30th October 2005
2. Michael A. Clemens and Todd J. Moss, *Ghost of 0.7%: origins and relevance of the international aid target*, Working Paper 68, September 2005, Center for Global Development
3. www.unicef.org.uk/unicef/polices/policy.detail.asp?policy=13
4. *Deutsche Welle* at http://206.532.133.22/hoc/Headline.aspx
5. quoted in European Scrutiny Committee 23rd report of session 2007-08, House of Commons published 23rd May 2008 p6
6. Fears are mounting that malaria will spread to develop countries too, e.g. "Climatic shifts are likely to enable some diseases and associated vectors--particularly mosquito-borne diseases such as malaria, yellow fever, and dengue--to spread to new areas. Warmer temperatures and increased rainfall already have expanded the geographic range of malaria to some highland areas in Sub-Saharan Africa and Latin America and could add several million more cases in developing country regions over the next two decades. The occurrence of waterborne diseases associated with temperature-sensitive environments, such as cholera, also is likely to increase." *The Global Infectious Disease Threat and Its Implications for the United States,* National Intelligence Estimate *NIE 99-17D, January 2000*. The Estimate was produced under the auspices of David F. Gordon, National Intelligence Officer for Economics and Global Issues. http://www.fas.org/irp/threat/nie99-17d.htm
7. HM Treasury letter to Environmental Audit Committee 17th December 2002
8. FBF Infofax, Summer 2002 at www.plasticbag.com
9. HM Treasury letter, op cit
10. *Outflanked: The World Trade Organisation, International Trade and Sustainable Development*, Eleventh report of session 2005-06, Environmental Audit Committee, House of Commons, 23rd November 2006 p. Ev 19
11. *ibid* p.31
12. *Growth isn't working: The unbalanced distribution of benefits and costs from economic growth*, nef, January 2006
13. Nicholas Stern, *The Economics of Climate Change: The Stern Review*, Cambridge University Press, 2006 p.xvi
14. *ibid* p.239
15. see for example "Carbon Output Must Near Zero To Avert Danger, New Studies Say" in the *Washington Post*, 10th March 2008
16. Joseph Stiglitz and Linda Bilmes, *The Three Trillion Dollar War: The true cost of the Iraq conflict*, Allen Lane, London 2008
17. Environmental Audit Committee, Reaching an international agreement on climate change, House of Commons, HC335, 2008 evidence page 103
18. *The ethical consumerism report 2007*, Co-operative Bank http://www.co-operativebanl.co.uk/images/pdf/ethical_consumer_report_2007.pdf
19. Adair Turner in Andrew Simms and Joe Smith (eds) *Do Good Lives Have to Cost the Earth?* Constable and Robinson, London, 2008, p.95
20. *Wall Street Journal Europe*, 4th/6th April, 2008
21. *Guardian*, 26th June 2008
22. http://www.euractiv.com/en/sustainability/interview-us-james-connaughton-climate-change-policy/article-140336
23. *Financial Times*, 23rd November 2005

3

a fair COP

> *We will not solve this problem if we do not each take our share of the responsibility for tackling it. Nobody can protect themselves from climate change unless we protect each other by building a global basis for climate security. This goes to the heart of the UN's mission. And the UN must be at the heart of the solution. To put it starkly, if we all try to free ride, we will all end up in free fall, with accelerating climate change the result of our collective failure to respond in time to this shared threat. Look just at the danger posed by rising sea levels: potentially this could cause massive damage to some of the key urban centres of our global civilization: London, Shanghai, Dhaka, Singapore, Amsterdam, Cairo, and – yes - Manhattan - all are at risk.*

Foreign Secretary Margaret Beckett [1]

A great unsung success of the UN climate change process is the requirement on all countries to maintain national GHG inventories, which have to be reported through the UNFCCC to the international community. And although the accuracy of these reports inevitably varies, there have been improvements which allow for better and more effective GHG emission monitoring and reduction activities to take place. A visit to the UNFCCC's website reveals all. Here we find how G8 countries like Canada, Italy, Japan and the United States have all increased their emissions against the 1990 baseline.[2] Canada's is by far the worst record with an increase of over 54 per cent. In this respect the new Canadian Conservative Prime Minister, Stephen Harper could with some justification abandon previous Liberal commitments to tackling climate change, since none of them seemed to be working. But with Canada's new tar sands gold rush in full swing it seems unlikely that we will see any significant change there soon, even despite a softening of Harper's rhetoric and the seismic regime change in the United States, breaking what Al Gore once described as the 'Bush/Harper Administration.'

On the plus side, the UK, France, and Germany have all made reductions against the 1990 baseline, contributing to an overall EU reduction of four per cent. The other G8 country, the Russian Federation too has made a reduction – 1990 representing the beginning of the dismantling of a lot of heavy, carbon emitting industry – rather than the beginning of an enlightened drive to reduce GHG emissions. If it were a matter of climate change policy, then Latvia with a reduction of 161.5 per cent would carry away the global prize for doing the most and we would all be flocking to Riga to learn how it was done. The fact is, the UNFCCC's chart of Annex One countries' GHG emissions reveals a distinct lack of evidence of coherence or design in the way the signatories to Kyoto have sought to address climate change.

Let's imagine if you wanted to build a house, who would you see first? An architect or a builders' merchant? It might be very tempting to choose the builders' merchant so as to see immediately the materials you would need to commence building and to get a feel for them. Perhaps even to see if there were any special offers or cut-price bargains. Or you could leave it to the builders' merchant alone to tell you what you needed, in which case you might run the risk of being offloaded with a large quantity of surplus and outdated materials which nobody else wanted. Then, how would you put them together to get the optimum result? It would be far more sensible to visit an architect first, to ensure that your requirements could be planned and executed properly. You would be far more in control if you worked from the design which fitted your needs.

This may be an inexact analogy for the approach we need to take to address climate change, but it suffices to illustrate an essential point: any climate change framework must show how the pieces fit together, how they contribute to the solution, and what is needed of each. The bottom line for this piece of intelligent design is that it must demonstrably solve the problem faster than we're creating it.

We are as yet stumbling around the builders' yard, rather than working with the architect. We can see lots of technological wizardry, much of it unproven, as is the case for example with carbon capture and storage. Much new technology is indeed impressive, and will play a vital role. Yet the pieces will not deliver the result without the design – and it is a design which has been more or less readily available in outline form since 191 countries signed the Rio Earth Summit declaration establishing the United Nations Framework Convention on Climate Change (UNFCCC) in 1992. Article 2 says:

> The ultimate objective of this Convention and any related legal instruments that the Conference of the Parties may adopt is

to achieve, in accordance with the relevant provisions of the Convention, stabilisation of greenhouse gas concentrations in the atmosphere at a level that would prevent dangerous anthropogenic interference with the climate system.[3]

Article 3(1) says:

The Parties should protect the climate system for the benefit of present and future generations of humankind, on the basis of equity and in accordance with their common but differentiated responsibilities and respective capabilities. Accordingly, the developed country Parties should take the lead in combating climate change and the adverse effects thereof.[4]

Sometimes it seems impudent to have to re-iterate these fundamental points, but in the 17 years since the UNFCCC was ratified, confusion rather than the clarity expressed in these articles has characterised the subsequent process. It wasn't as if the UNFCCC represented unwelcome thinking at the time. President George Bush Snr., in a speech from his 1988 presidential campaign said:

Those who think we're powerless to do anything about the greenhouse effect are forgetting about the White House effect. As President I intend to do something about it. I will convene a global conference on climate change.....all nations will be welcome - and indeed, all nations will be needed.[5]

From those UNFCCC articles two over-arching principles emerge which are essential in any final framework. There has to be a *stabilisation of greenhouse gas concentrations in the atmosphere at a level that would prevent dangerous anthropogenic interference with the climate system and we should protect the climate system for the benefit of present and future generations of humankind, on the basis of equity and in accordance with their common but differentiated responsibilities and respective capabilities . .* And in the words of George Bush Snr., "all nations will be needed."

Naturally, there must be a huge doubt as to whether 191 nations, including the United States, in 1992 still run by Bush Snr. would have signed up to the UNFCCC if they had thought it was going to be mandatory. Some nations probably signed up solely on the grounds that it didn't mean they really had to do anything. That does not diminish the principles established in the UNFCCC, but in the minds of some it meant the Convention was just another UN fudge, a statement of wishful or woolly thinking. Such a response may be unsurprising coming from climate change sceptics, but it would also loom large in the minds of those whose ideology would be shaken to the core by any reference to 'equity' or even worse, inter- or intra-generational responsibility.

The climate change deniers now inhabit much the same space as flat-earthers, and their objections can be dealt with by reference to the evidence. The harder, more resilient resistance to the principles of the UNFCCC emerges from our economic worldview, with its narrow anthropocentric concept of growth, moreover a concept of growth which has historically excluded and still excludes vast numbers of people from its benefits. The excluded peoples of the world have little reason to invest hope in solutions which emerge from the old model. UN Secretary General Ban Ki-moon wrote:

Put bluntly, solutions to global warming proposed by developed nations cannot come at the expense of less fortunate neighbours on the planet. How else would we achieve our Millennium Development Goals of halving world poverty, so solemnly laid down at previous G-8 meetings, if the developing world's aspirations for a greater stake in global prosperity are not honoured?[6]

Neither of the UNFCCC core principles can be revoked. We cannot exceed the limit (greenhouse gas stabilisation level) climate change imposes; nor can we avoid developing some system of distributing responsibilities in order to stay within that limit. The latter principle, which the UNFCCC says should be based on equity, is the principle of climate justice. The first principle is the easiest to define, since there is considerable agreement between nations about the science of climate change. The real difficulty is dividing up the responsibility for addressing it. The are two distinct approaches as indicated in the analogy of building a house – we either have an architectural framework which has a clear metric, or we have a collection of separate elements and our fingers crossed. It is quite conceivable that both approaches could fail. Firstly because nobody was prepared to will the means to complete the design and secondly simply because without a design, nobody knew whether their components added up, even though in their own discreet ways they each added something of value.

So far, the merchant's yard approach has been taken and everyone knows that it doesn't add up. The Kyoto Protocol, proposing a five per cent cut in GHG emissions by 2012 against a 1990 baseline was clearly not enough, but was accepted as being the only realistic starting point. Deputy Prime Minister

John Prescott, who was acting as the UK's lead negotiator (and as the UK was president of the EU at that time, Prescott also spoke on behalf of the EU) described the haphazard nature of the Kyoto talks as being like an 'enormous jigsaw puzzle,' "The main countries were each offering to accept different rates of reductions, but at the same time they were worried about what other countries would accept, saying they wouldn't do it if the others weren't doing the same, or if they were offering to accept less."[7] Perhaps the jigsaw analogy is more apt than building a house, since what Kyoto produced was a far from complete jigsaw. As Prescott noted, "What it boiled down to in the end was that I got Japan to settle for a figure, as long as it was less than the USA's. The USA would agree a figure, as long as it was less than Europe's."[8] Kyoto could be hailed a success because something was agreed, even if it was only getting people around the table to attempt the jigsaw puzzle. It was not about willing the means, as Bill Clinton made clear. He wanted "an agreement we could sign, with firm targets but without undue restrictions on how to achieve them."[9] This was despite his earlier ambition that strongly favoured "setting aggressive targets for the reduction of greenhouse gas emissions."[10] The sticking point was ensuring that both developed and developing countries (particularly China and India) were part of the deal. In the end, the Protocol was not even presented to Congress, since President Clinton didn't believe it would be accepted if it were not inclusive of the developing world, and indeed a Senate resolution at the time opposing it on these grounds received almost unanimous support.

On top of Kyoto's omission of the developing world, and the absence of ambition in the target agreed, there were other important omissions – the most significant of these perhaps being the exclusion of aviation and shipping. These are amongst the fastest growing sectors for GHG emissions, but to have tried to include them at Kyoto would probably have overloaded the delegates. Nobody had a model of how to count aviation and shipping GHG emissions and other international bodies were left with the responsibility of looking at their environmental impacts, which is to say the issue was kicked into the long grass.

To what extent have these omissions been addressed, 12 years later? Can we expect all the pieces of the jigsaw to be in place in Copenhagen in 2009 – which will determine the post-Kyoto treaty? It is hard to see. Professor Michael Grubb, chief economist at the Carbon Trust and a member of the government's Climate Change Committee said after the 2008 G8 summit "There's a very big gap between the rhetoric of consensus about the size of the problem and the need for reductions, and the lack of anything specific that will make any difference. One can see five pages of text – I'm not sure I can see a single thing that's actually going to reduce emissions."[11]

The barrier to action is competition. Nobody wants to see their economy damaged by another's which itself does not face the extra costs of reducing GHG emissions. But the twin track approach to the resolution of global trade disparities – through the WTO's Doha 'Development' Round of negotiations – and the resolution of climate change through the UNFCCC is fundamentally incapable of resolving the competition issue, but is instead merely making matters worse. Indeed, in late 2005, when the two fora were slogging away at the same time at their conflicting agendas, the WTO in Hong Kong and the UNFCCC in Montreal, they blithely ignored each other.

The resolution to the problem is widely held to be the creation of a global market in GHG emissions, building largely on the

European Union ETS. If every country can trade its emissions, then we will have a market solution to the 'greatest market failure of all time.' By August, 2008 progress towards this goal could be reported, as the UN and the EU concluded a testing phase of the merger of the EU ETS and UN's Clean Development Mechanism (CDM), one if its 'flexible mechanisms' created at Kyoto. "This now paves the way for the transfer of credits from the Clean Development Mechanism into the EU registry system. Linking up with the UN's carbon credit registry will further strengthen Europe's leading role in the global carbon market" said EU Environment Commissioner, Stavros Dimas.[12] Eventually, other emerging emissions trading schemes could be allowed into the system, such as the Regional Greenhouse Gas Initiative started in 2008 by several north eastern states in the US, or a proposed ETS in Australia. Obviously, if emissions trading is to have any chance of success it has to be global, but is that a sufficient quality of success? Far from it. Indeed, without significant improvements, emissions trading could undermine all our efforts to tackle climate change. There needs to be a far greater degree of honesty amongst proponents of emissions trading if these improvements are to be made.

The first question that must be asked of the ETS route to emissions reduction is whether it operates as a framework based market or if it has become a market based framework. At present, emission trading schemes have all the qualities of the latter, since they do not define the solution, they are but a mechanism that has become a substitute for the solution – an activity whose contribution suffers infamously from leakage and imprecision. ETS allows for all sorts of false claims to be made. One of the cardinal falsehoods is to overstate the reductions ETS makes. Here is an example of how ETS acts as a political placebo, through the simple mistake of double counting its benefits. The following exchange took place between Tim Yeo MP, Chairman of the House of Commons Environmental Audit Committee, and Malcolm Wicks MP, Energy Minister, during an inquiry into CCS and the proposed Kingsnorth coal fired power plant:

> *Mr Yeo:* If the government is so keen on CCS and making such excellent progress towards it why on earth is it even contemplating authorising the construction of a coal-fired power station before we have the technology?
>
> *Mr Wicks:* There are mechanisms in place. I am thinking of the European Union's emissions trading scheme of which we are fully a part. The objective of the ETS is to help us across Europe to hit the very demanding CO_2 reduction targets. The mechanism of the ETS is to bear down on carbon emissions over time. That means anyone contemplating a new fossil fuel power station will have to take that into account in terms of the economics and take steps to reduce carbon emissions.[13]

Here then the minister is claiming that E-On, the plant's operator will have to purchase carbon credits to pay for the emissions they produce in the absence of CCS. Thus, the plant will be rendered carbon neutral. This would be fine, except that DBERR's viewpoint does not exactly square with Defra's, which in response to a question in an earlier EAC inquiry said: "As developing country Parties always correctly point out, they reduce greenhouse gas emissions in their countries by participating in the Clean Developing Mechanism."[14] Thus, our coal fired power station's carbon emission reductions are also being claimed by others. On whose carbon balance sheet should they appear? If we are to avoid double counting, they can only appear once.

Another problem arises depending on the timing of the delivery of the actual carbon reducing performance of the credits, or the problem of future accounting. This occurs when today's carbon intensive activity is to be offset by an emissions reducing activity like planting trees, which will take years or decades to mop up an equivalent amount of carbon emissions. Clearly, given the IPCC's very tight timetable to peak and then reduce our emissions by 2015, we need to ensure that the equivalent savings in GHGs happens concurrently. Then there is the problem of whether the carbon reducing activity was going to happen anyway, that is whether the ETS or CDM brought additionality – the avoidance of extra emissions which could not have been avoided but for the trading element. With much of the CDM to date, there is an abundance of evidence to show for example that hydro-electricity schemes that were already in the pipeline or even in the process of being built with sufficient existing finance, later attracted CDM credits. A host of similar problems can easily be dredged up, making the offsetting of Kingsnorth's carbon emissions a very dodgy proposition. Without an overarching framework to which the markets answer – rather than the other way round – any claim made on behalf of ETS at best is meaningless and at worst is downright dangerous, since ETS actually slows down the rate at which we eliminate carbon intensive activities. This is perhaps the most difficult to overcome of all the charges against carbon markets made by their opponents.

Even if it were true that the carbon market finds a genuinely equivalent (and additional) reduction of GHGs for a continued carbon activity, it remains the case that the whole deal will be predicated on the notion that the carbon reduction activity will be cheaper than fixing or stopping the source of the original GHG emissions. This is the market's 'least cost efficiency' paradigm which is so attractive to those whose budgets are under pressure. The phrase that 'it doesn't matter where in the world the CO_2 comes from, a tonne of it anywhere is just as damaging' gives the impression that preventing that tonne for €20 in Zambia is better than preventing it for €30 in Europe. But all this actually means is that we will continue on our carbon intensive path at less cost to ourselves, so perpetuating the very thing we claim to be stopping. In the context of the UK, the perpetuating aspect of this argument reared its head in the debates over the Climate Change Act, where the tradable element of what is known as the 'net UK carbon account' was at issue. Should we allow ourselves the privilege of telling the world that we will cut our CO_2 emissions by 60 per cent or 80 per cent, when we may include in that figure perhaps 30 per cent of carbon credits bought in? Shouldn't what we do to help the developing world avoid carbonising their economies be extra?

Given the devoted adherence to carbon markets that has now gripped the political and financial establishments, one has to pray that these flaws in carbon markets are not fatal since if they are, we will have wasted many years on a worthless activity. The objections should be engaged with, not dismissed, and crucially, until they are addressed and fixed we should not be permitted to claim that the carbon markets are working, since that merely induces a false sense of security. It also eases the pressure to use other methods like taxation and regulation which as Bill Clinton noted in his memoir My Life, are unlikely to prove popular.

Another issue which cannot be avoided and which markets have no interest in, is whether carbon trading as it is currently configured is the best way 'to deliver equity,' referred to in UNFCCC Article 3(1) quoted above. The efficiency-at-least-cost route determines that an avoided African tonne of CO_2 is likely to be cheaper than an avoided European tonne of CO_2. Therefore, we can delay taking action even though we created the problem in the first place, and our money will find the cheapest get out of jail card it can find. But why should an avoided tonne of African CO_2 be cheaper? Probably because employment costs are lower, because land values are less and because the infrastructure is less developed – there are fewer 'replacement' costs associated with ending one activity and starting another. But ironically, Africa has seen the least benefit from the carbon markets, with fewer CDM projects being given approval than anywhere else. In other words, they are so poor nobody believes they're capable of generating the extra CO_2 which could then be avoided. 'Lack of infrastructure' means that many African countries cannot even climb on to the bottom rung of the market's ladder.

Hence we have a market-based framework which is not delivering the emissions reductions it should in order to warrant the primary position it holds in policy making, but nor is it delivering the equitable solution to climate change which was at the core of the UNFCCC's objectives. Is this situation going to improve by osmosis, through some marvellous incremental transformation, or by introducing some irreducible principles which will discipline climate change negotiators and keep them focussed on what has to happen? What does have to happen?

In order to win the support of all countries that are party to the UNFCCC there surely needs to be a firmer expression of the equity principle than has hitherto been provided. Too many speeches from G8 and UN podiums have commenced with an acknowledgement of the desirability of an equitable outcome, but from the same platforms other promises have been made and not kept for all to see. There are undoubtedly many difficulties with the issue of equity. Nick Stern grappled with these in his original report and found the answer hard to pin down, but has subsequently argued that "Meeting a 500ppmv CO_2e target requires a cut in all GHG emissions of around 50% by 2050, relative to 1990 emission levels, and further cuts after that. This would imply – as a matter of simple arithmetic – a commitment to per capita emissions by 2050 of around 2T CO_2e as a world average, with little scope for significant deviation." (emphasis added)[15] Thus the simple arithmetic tells us where we have to go, what has to happen. But the simple arithmetic eludes most climate change negotiators, perhaps for the very reason that they don't want to go there. Developed country governments, whose citizens enjoy 10 to 20 tonne CO_2 lifestyles, have so far proven unable to grapple with such a demanding metric. Developing countries, many of whose citizens are already at or below two tonnes CO_2 each, fear entrapment in poverty with the developed world once again not delivering on its promises but instead relying on a market which has lined the pockets of a few operators for a dubious climate change gain.

The conclusion Stern has been inching towards sounds a little like the proposal for a climate change framework which has been doing the rounds for over 15 years. Devised by the Global Commons Institute's director Aubrey Meyer, Contraction and Convergence (C&C) has become, in the words of Professor Sir David King the "buzz phrase on many negotiators' lips."[16]

Sadly, it seems to have remained just a buzz. In essence C&C proposes a contraction of GHG emissions – which almost everyone agrees with – and an eventual convergence to a per capita level of emissions, globally. C&C hardens up the UNFCCC's objectives, and provides a comprehensive metric on how to achieve them. Perhaps this is what so frightens the negotiators – their tiresome obfuscations, delays and Aunt Sallies are all exposed to what Stern called 'simple arithmetic.' Even critics of C&C have had to concede its essential logic. Whilst the World Resources Institute (WRI) asserts that "International agreements predicated on equal per capita emission entitlements are unlikely to garner consensus" it is however "important to note that the implementation of virtually any national or international climate change policies is likely to have the effect of promoting a convergence in per capita emission levels over time. Considering that over the long term net emissions must fall to zero, convergence is a corollary of climate protection."[17] According to the WRI's authors, the reason why commitments to convergence won't find agreement is because of the disparate sizes of national economies and populations and their current carbon footprints – and yet it seems that an equitable outcome will necessarily be a corollary of the result of climate change policies. Perhaps negotiators are blind to this inevitable result, and don't feel bound to make it happen. If that is the case, maybe it is because some of them want to argue for a permanently unfair slice of the cake, in which case any framework they come up with will be just as insufficient as Kyoto was.

But perhaps there is another explanation. Professor Tom Burke, giving evidence to the EAC's inquiry into reaching an international agreement on climate change, said

I do think that contraction and convergence is an outcome of solving the problem, not an input to solving the problem. The idea that we can solve this problem by agreeing some mechanism that . . set out to share out the per capita burden is frankly very idealistic but I am not sure it is very practical. If you cannot get people to agree to things that we are already suggesting are difficult and will take you nowhere near a contract and converge situation, why would you think they would agree to something that is a lot more difficult and even harder to work out how you are going to deliver? Personally I am pretty sceptical about contract and converge. Any of these ideas are fundamentally about how you share the burden. When your discourse is about burden sharing, people retreat into saying 'you first, me later' and what you have to do is get to a mode where the conversation is 'me too.'[18]

The convergence conversation is the biggest 'me too' dialogue one could wish for – it might indeed also address the question 'Am I in?' - and could permit the space that Burke yearns for, but his long experience of climate change negotiations has, as perhaps it might with any regular attendee, enveloped him in a 'can't see the wood for the trees' perspective. We should be asking ourselves how it is possible that anyone travelling these days to a UN climate conference might be repelled by the 'simple arithmetic' of Stern or the WRI? Are we to believe that only a minority of participants in the negotiations have been issued with special 3D spectacles that let them see what is around the corner? One of Defra's lead 'sherpa' at the Bali conference was Chris Dodwell, and he told the same EAC inquiry that "were the UK to come forward with an ideal proposal of 'This is what an international framework should look like,' that is the surest guarantee that we will not achieve it. We are not in a position where we can effectively put forward a framework. The reality of the negotiations is that countries are now developing their own ideas about what action they are willing to take."[19] It seems that anyone who proposes a framework will be risking their diplomatic reputation. Thus we end up with the teamwork spirit of a poker game, a game which is more rather than less likely to let the weaker hand win.

So the whole process becomes concerned with simply managing an ad hoc selection of tasks – rather than dividing up the whole problem into manageable tasks and seeing how they can be put together to solve the whole problem. Discussions in the first week of each UN COP conference set the tone with agonisingly technocratic examinations of the detailed work of the COP – the wrong end of the telescope comes to mind. The second week, which is largely given over to short statements from senior politicians provides a grandstanding opportunity but one which has already been determined by the process of wading through the horrendous detail of the previous week. Of course, the detailed analysis and preparation is important, but because nobody wants to risk their diplomatic reputation on staking out a clear overarching framework, the details are allowed to overpower a greater, radical vision, and very importantly it disables any yardstick by which to measure the sufficiency of the whole process. The academics Gwyn Prins and Steve Rayner put their finger on it when they wrote:

> Although the rational thing to do in the face of a bad investment is to cut your losses, get out and try something different, there are many obstacles that may prevent this, ranging from administrative inconvenience, to psychological and emotional

barriers. It is difficult to abandon profound investments not just of capital, but also of effort and conviction, or of reputation and status. Therefore, as well as it being administratively inconvenient, politicians and diplomats who have invested much personal effort and conviction in creating the Kyoto regime may simply find it psychologically and emotionally impossible to walk away from an entrenched community of understanding and action to which they fell they belong and that belongs to them. Meeting inside the special bubble and breathing the rarefied air of international summitry reinforces both sorts of feelings.[20]

Something has to emerge from this bubble, and perhaps this helps explain the Kyoto culture of 'projectitis' whereby participants gain credibility by successfully pushing forward their pet projects. This culture appeals to both developed and developing world countries. Developed world participants – not least the NGOs – want to come away parading their golden trophies to show their various audiences how successful they've been. They cannot admit failure, since voters and/or members might question their abilities. Developing countries, long since weary of broken promises want tangible projects delivered too, since the principle of a bird in the hand is far more valuable to their domestic audiences – and for some of those audiences inevitably, a project could mean the difference between life and death. There would be nothing wrong with this culture if it submitted itself to an overarching analysis which could tell us whether it led to an overall result of which we could be satisfied. But it doesn't – it is more like the philosophical conundrum which posits that to get from A to B you have to first traverse half the distance, and so on in an infinite regression meaning you never arrive at the destination since there will always be half of something left to cross.

If, as we have heard, the rather inevitable outcome of the UNFCCC process will resemble a C&C outcome, shouldn't we trust that this will simply happen – either through an iterative, arithmetical process – or perhaps merely as an unintended though desirable consequence? And would it make any difference how we got there, so long as we got there? There is an argument that to make C&C an explicit outcome is to frighten the horses of capitalism, since it is felt that since an obvious underlying purpose of C&C is egalitarian, namely that it would confer a right to per capita carbon emissions by a certain date, this is an artificial 'right' which is unjustifiably proscriptive when it is conceivable that there are other ways we could arrive at a satisfactorily carbon constrained world. Nick Stern, having rejected the argument that per capita emissions rights are the same as democratic rights has now nevertheless begun to use the phrase 'pragmatic rights' which avoids getting hung up on definitional issues, or bogged down with a proposition which appears to assert that we may all have an equal economic right of any description. It is that last proposition which makes negotiators tremble so, since they fear that the rich will run a mile if they even get a scent of it. In addition, beyond references to ending slavery, the right to equal pay and to own property, the UN Universal Declaration of Human Rights (UDHR) has little to say about economic rights, and nothing at all about environmental rights, if such things exist.

Nick Stern has found another objection that takes matters to another extreme. "Asserting equal rights to pollute or emit seems to me to have a very shady ethical grounding. Emissions deeply damage and sometimes kill others. Do we have a "right" to do so?"[21] Currently this question is answered in the moot mode, since we simply do it anyway and take it for granted. Indeed it would be hard not to, since all human beings exhale about 1kg of CO_2 each a day.[22] Perhaps fat people exhale a little bit more. But at least the CO_2 in human breath is carbon neutral, since it does not exceed the CO_2 which has already been absorbed by plants (this prompts another argument for being a vegetarian, as veggies may not be responsible for killing so many others given the higher embedded levels of CO_2 in meat production, as IPCC chair Dr Rajendra Pachuari pointed out in the summer of 2008). Stern's implication that the C&C approach might provide the basis for legalised genocide is thus a little awry. Since by the laws of nature there will never be a time when human activity ceases to be carbon based in one form or another, it seems a little parsimonious to deny any human a right to emit carbon.

But there is the question of whether all people actually deserve equal 'carbon rights.' This problem has been forcefully expressed by a former Indian Environment Minister Kamal Nath (and now Commerce and Industry minister), who wrote to fellow COP delegates at their first meeting in 1995:

We unequivocally reject the theory that the monetary value of people's lives around the world is different because the value imputed should be proportional to the disparate income levels of the potential victims concerned. Developing countries have no - indeed negative - responsibility for causing global climate change. Yet they are being blamed for possible future impacts, although historical impacts by industrialised economies are being regarded as water-under-the-bridge or "sunk costs" in the jargon of these biased economists. To compound the problem, global damage assessments are being expressed in US dollar equivalent. Thus the monetary significance of damages to developing countries is substantially under-represented. Damage to human beings, whether in developed or developing countries, must be treated as equal, and cannot be translated in terms of the existing currency exchange rate systems.[23]

Convergence as an intended aim suggests, unlike most of the rights in the UDHR, that one day there should be at least one form of absolute resource equality between humans, as opposed to a civic right or a right of opportunity. The mere suggestion that a human may have a right to a resource is anathema to those who are now so keen to create this new carbon commodity and put a price on it. They confuse wealth and resources. Despite the claims of many senior politicians (starting with George W. Bush) that economic growth can occur with reducing carbon intensity, which if taken to its logical conclusion could mean living in a world of entirely decarbonised wealth, they nevertheless feel that stating that too boldly may offend the current economic model. Rather than tackling this confusion by setting out a clear road map for decarbonised wealth, they cling to the fear of losing wealth. As Nath's letter shows, as things stand (there has been little change in official policies since 1995) one individual's worth may not even be measured in the same way, ironically leaving those who have the most wealth and the most responsibility for the problem arguing for a biased methodology which is all about preserving their advantage. The process of decarbonising wealth thus becomes a victim of an irrational fear which prevents a speedier adoption of its remedy. If all countries permit themselves to take only the actions that 'they are willing to take' on the assumption that that is the best way to protect their economies, then the resulting hodge-podge approach to climate change will guarantee a rising tide that sinks all boats. The further irony of that is that developed country economies, being more highly valued, have more to lose, and it will be interesting to see how resilient they are to those losses.

The C&C model ensures that countries' actions can be measured against each other within the one and only atmospheric envelope we have. If one country contributes more or less to the solution, other countries can synchronise their behaviour accordingly in an integral path. This is not to say they would be encouraged to do less because another is doing more, but such a system encourages a better understanding of relative responsibilities. Regardless of what Tom Burke says about the implicit negativity of the language of burden sharing, there is no getting around it. When one punches a pillow, it always comes out somewhere else, and as we seek to reduce the overall size of the pillow we simply have to know who is punching it and on whose account the consequent bulge will appear. The climate pillow is no more than a finite envelope, but to date we have been talking as if extra little bits could be sewn on every time some country or other says how difficult this all is.

What if to meet the objections of those who resist the convergence by design approach, we said we'll just pursue contraction alone? The final outcome would be the same anyway, they say. Would this aid the negotiators, allowing them more flexibility? We could do away with the formal aspect of burden sharing, and leave it to people to simply suggest different mechanisms to reduce carbon emissions. (It should be said that C&C itself allows any manner of mechanisms to achieve its ends.) This is essentially a continuation of the pragmatic approach which has operated to date (driven by some very undemanding targets), though no doubt we would want to see more effective mechanisms put in place. Putting aside the fact that the pragmatic approach has so far failed rather miserably to reduce GHG emissions, it has nevertheless to a limited extent mitigated the growth in emissions. We have to go much further than that, so what is emerging which will deliver? Since C&C's detractors often say that C&C is politically unrealistic, we are entitled to ask what is the politically realistic alternative which will guide policy making? So far, the only answer has been a desperate shout of 'realpolitick!' More of the same, except maybe tougher. Tighter rhetoric, but no metric please – we know what the scientists tell us, but in the real world of politics there has to be wriggle room.

Hence, the development of carbon markets will continue apace, and their efficacy will probably improve – to what extent is anybody's guess. This will be the single most sought-out result of the Copenhagen talks, a result that will have to be sufficiently nuanced to allow the new US administration to make a rapid accession to a leadership role. Since everyone since the days of Kyoto has been waiting for the US to take a leadership role, all eyes will be on what the new President has to offer – and can get through Congress. If history is anything to go by, then even if Congress is in a more open mood to signing a new climate change treaty, it will still want to ensure that all countries are party to it. It seems highly unlikely that in a world beset by economic woes that members of Congress would agree to sign anything which carries any hint of a competitive burden on their home state and its hard pressed workforce. This debate is already raging between states that have signed up to their own inter-state carbon trading schemes – it will intensify once foreign elements are introduced. Such arguments are not insoluble, but what compromises will be made settling them? Without a metric such as that provided by C&C, any compromise will appear permissible. The biggest compromise of all would be to say yes to convergence, but at a level cheekily suggested by the Indian government which committed India 'not to emit more GHGs per capita then the developed world.' This places the ball firmly in the developed world's court, and exposes much of the self-serving dialogue we have perpetuated for fear of losing our 'leadership' role. It is sometimes a complete mystery as to how climate change conference delegates from the developing world can keep a straight face when colleagues from the north talk of equity. These conflicting pressures have to be reconciled if a new treaty is to work. Who in the developing world is going to sign away their fair share if they cannot see how it delivers the endgame – or at worst delays it?

It is curious that the British government is so coy in espousing the C&C approach, since it is that very framework which underpins the Climate Change Act. In coming up with an initial target of at least a 60 per cent cut in carbon dioxide emissions, the government looked to a report of the Royal Commission on Environmental Pollution (RCEP), published in 2000, called Energy – The Changing Climate.[24] One of the report's recommendations, and the government's response, delivered in February, 2003 shows how infuriatingly consistent the government has been in its characteristic 'open mindedness:'

(Recommendation Three) The Government should press for a future global climate agreement based on the contraction and convergence approach, combined with international trading in emission permits. Together, these offer the

best long-term prospect of securing equity, economy and international consensus.

(*Response*) The Government is keen to establish a dialogue on possible approaches to future target-setting. However, the Global Commons Institute's contraction and convergence approach is only one of a number of potential models for global agreement on addressing greenhouse gas emissions, some of which may be more attractive to developing countries and still promote the objectives that we are striving to fulfill. Other possible approaches include, for example, setting dynamic targets linked to GDP, or setting limits on the basis of countries' historical emissions (the "Brazilian Proposal"). The Government believes that it would be premature to rule out any options at this stage and plans to engage constructively in future debates. There is likely to be an increasing emphasis on the evolution of commitments under the Kyoto Protocol following its entry into force. In any discussion on this matter, it will be important to take into account the views of developing countries since agreements are reached by consensus.[25]

That was five years ago and still nothing has been ruled in or out, as the wheels of international diplomacy crank round and round. The author of the response may have wondered whether a consensus could have been built around something which by 2003 had already received endorsements from around the globe, not least from the developing countries so patronizingly referred to in the response. But criticism on this point has to be tempered by the knowledge that our own (and much vaunted) Climate Change Act uses the same methodology as the RCEP report to arrive at a target for emissions cuts, and to any informed observer this fact must be laden with meaning. Perhaps the government's apparent open-mindedness is really just a bit of a bluff, in an attempt to 'establish a dialogue' (within a dialogue that in UNFCCC terms is already more than 10 years old). At some point however, somebody is bound to ask of our GHG reduction target 'how did you work that out then?' – and the ministerial equivalent of coughing and spluttering will not do.

Producing a national Climate Change Act in response to a global problem was always going to throw up these difficulties, and although there has been obfuscation over the role in it of C&C, the Act can still deservedly be called groundbreaking. It will be especially groundbreaking if government departments are forced to translate it into their policies. It is very difficult to see how those departments most tied to the historical model of economic growth are going to cope with it. To put it unkindly, we do not want to see our environment minister waving in his or her hand another piece of well-intentioned but useless, ignorable paper declaring 'peace in our time.' This will almost certainly be the case if the current market model is allowed to remain the pre-eminent driver of emissions reductions. In delivering the Act's targets, more has to be done to strengthen its carbon budgeting powers and to rule the markets with an iron discipline.

Notes

1. UN General Assembly 25th September 2006 http://www.fco.gov.uk/en/newsroom/latest-news/?view=Speech&id=1893381
2. http://unfccc.int/files/inc/graphics/image/gif/graph4_2007_ori.gif
3. http://unfccc.int/essential_background/convention/background/items/1353.php
4. http://unfccc.int/essential_background/convention/background/items/1355.php
5. Quoted in *The Greenhouse Effect*, Stewart Boyle and John Ardill, 1989. Bush Snr's concerns for a fully global approach were more recently endorsed by the UK's former Chief Scientific Advisor, Prof. Sir David King who told the Environmental Audit Committee (12th June 2007): "What happens to global markets if only the developed countries reach an agreement on cap and trade and meeting the obligations? We would see naturally from the economics an export of the smokestack industries, the heavy manufacturing industries, to the countries that are not signed up and we would certainly see the trade in farming, particularly livestock farming, also moving to those areas. That is precisely why it is critically important that we have a global agreement. The agreement cannot work if we exclude half the countries of the world, so it is

absolutely critical that we have a global agreement."

6. *International Herald Tribune*, 4th June 2007

7. John Prescott, *Prezza: Pulling No Punches*, Headline, London 2008 p.223

8. *ibid* p.225

9. Bill Clinton, My Life, Hutchinson, London 2004 p.770

10. *ibid* p.767

11. www.guardian.co.uk/environment/2008/jul/10/climatechnage.carbonemissions/

12. http://www.edie.net/news/news_story.asp?id=15113

13. http://www.publications.parliament.uk/pa/cm200708/cmselect/cmenvaud/uc654-i/uc65402.htm

14. (Memorandum from Defra to EAC inquiry *Post Kyoto: The international context for progress on climate change*)

15. Nicholas Stern, *Key Elements of a Global Deal on Climate Change*, London School of Economic sand Political Science, 2008 p.8

16. Sir David King and Gabrielle Walker, *The Hot Topic: How to tackle global warming and still keep the lights on*, Bloomsbury, London 2008, p.188

17. Kevin A. Baumert, Timothy Herzog and Jonathan Pershing, Navigating the Numbers: Greenhouse Gas data and International Climate Policy, World Resouces Institute, Washington DC 2005 p.21

18. Environmental Audit Committee, *Reaching an international agreement on climate change*, House of Commons, 2008 p. Ev 47

19. *ibid* p. Ev 107

20. Gwyn Pris and Steve Rayner, *The Wrong Trousers: Radically Rethinking Climate Policy, James Martin Institute for Science and Civilization*, University of Oxford and the MacKinder Centre for the Study of Long-Wave Eevnts, London School of Economics, 2007 p.19

21. Nicholas Stern, the Richard T. Ely lecture, The Economics of Climate Change, *American Economic Review: Papers & Proceedings 2008, 98:2, –37* at http://www.aeaweb.org/articles.php?doi=10.1257/aer.98.2

22. http://www.gcrio.org/doctorgc/index.php/drweblog/C53/

23. quoted at www.gci.org.uk/articles/Nairob3b.pdf

24. Cm 4794, ISBN 0 10 147492 X, June 2000

25. www.defra.uk/government/rcep/pdf/rcep22_response.pdf

4

energy, or the want of it

Scientists have confirmed that enough solar energy falls on the surface of the earth every 40 minutes to meet 100 per cent of the entire world's energy needs for a full year.

Former Vice President Al Gore[1]

"91% of the energy coming out of the ground is lost or wasted before it becomes useful work. It does not have to be that way, not remotely. A glaring example is that half the input energy in central power plants goes up the stack as waste heat because we can't move heat effectively any distance at all."

George David, CEO United Technologies[2]

With the price of fossil fuels spiralling ever upwards in 2008 the need for a coherent energy policy bore down with urgency on policy makers around the globe, but sadly any hopes that some coherence would emerge have had to be put on hold. High energy costs hurt all economies and the poorest countries the hardest. Angry demonstrations calling for the lowering of prices – through the only mechanism available to governments, the lowering of fuel duties and taxes - occurred across continents. The response by governments was not to reduce taxes, but demand that oil producers increase the flow; the response by oil companies was to examine how much more oil they could get their hands on.[3] For the remnants of the 'Seven Sisters', who are largely shut out of OPEC, it meant the accelerated exploitation of alternative oil reserves such as the tar sands of Alberta, and the extension of exploration into areas previously off-limits – the polar region offering much hope. I once asked an ExxonMobil executive how long he thought oil would last: his somewhat surprising answer was that the supply was infinite.[4] This points to Exxon's confidence that when the price of oil goes up, efficiencies will kick in which will allow us to continue using it for as long as we wish – and can afford to do so of course - even if the supply diminishes. Higher prices extend the life of existing reserves and make new ones more viable, so the supply will not diminish as quickly some anticipate. Tony Hayward, Chairman of BP confidently expects a business as usual oil supply to last another 41 years, conveniently a couple of generations beyond the present.[5]

The problem with this analysis – if it is intended to lead us to believe we will automatically witness greater energy efficiency and net GHG reductions - is that there is no evidence that it works in the real world and plenty of evidence to the contrary. Yes, efficiencies are continually being made in engine technology (and most other technologies too) but since the demand for technology does not remain static the efficiencies have never been enough to compensate for the growth in our use of energy dependent technologies. Following the 1970s oil price spikes, American cars did become more efficient. But when the price went down again, that merely meant that more people could afford to drive cars with bigger engines which were a little cheaper to run than they once might have been. Hence, whilst motor manufacturers love to tell the European Commission how they've cut the carbon emissions of individual models in their vehicle fleet - usually whilst lobbying to prevent ever tighter emissions controls – the carbon emissions from vehicle use continues to rise, since more cars are sold and more cars are travelling longer distances.[6] The market for energy intensive technologies will also grow exponentially as more people access them globally. Only a non-market intervention, such as the enforcement of carbon rationing could make immediate and serious inroads into the growth of carbon emissions. In the meantime, ExxonMobil's piece of elastic will be stretched until something breaks, since the pressure to continue meeting the demand of a growing market will always be too profitable to ignore. So, if the price of oil continues to rise, new (or revisited) technologies will become attractive, such as oil-from-coal transport fuels. The last great push for oil-from-coal came from the Nazis during the war, since they possessed no indigenous oil reserves themselves, but it was very expensive and needless to say very dirty. Prof. Sir David King, the government's former chief scientist identified this as one significant downside to high oil prices, when asked if in the climate change context we could expect a silver lining.[7] Another controversial consequence of the oil price rise has been the expansion of the bio-fuels market, with impacts on food prices, bio-diversity and climate change, given that some bio-fuels may actually contribute more GHGs over their full life cycle than petroleum.

Even in the absence of climate change it seems evident except perhaps to the most recidivist of oil executives, that global energy requirements are entering a new, almost unprecedented period of upheaval. So far as oil goes, there seems little consensus as to what has driven up prices nor what the response should be. An oil crisis summit called in June, 2008 by King Abdullah of Saudi Arabia sought to allay fears that OPEC itself was seeking to capitalise on high prices for despite their $3 trillion windfall, the Saudi government's spokesperson said "We have realised that oil prices really have increased to unjustifiable and unreasonable levels."[8] The only head of government to attend the Jeddah summit was Gordon Brown, who saw an opportunity to use the summit as a platform for promoting renewable energy and nuclear power, calling upon OPEC countries to use their vast wealth to invest in these technologies, even though neither renewables or nuclear would be able to solve the immediate problem of oil price rises, nor the longer term question of sustainable transport. But with angry road hauliers back home threatening to bring London to a standstill, any tenuous linkage must have appeared attractive if it could be portrayed as taking decisive action. What OPEC members will have made of Brown's call on them to invest in low carbon technologies must also be moot since Saudi Arabia had shown its unabashed colours at the UN Bali climate change conference the previous year by calling for compensation for lost oil revenues should a global climate deal reduce their fossil fuel income. It has not been OPEC members alone who have raked in billions of extra revenue from the oil price hike – the profits of the oil companies rose dramatically too, leading to calls for these to be subjected to a tax windfall profits. On this front the UK government has been less forthcoming, perhaps sharing the Financial Times' point of view that windfall taxes "undermine investment, unless a government can somehow credibly guarantee that the tax is a one-off levy. This is next to impossible, particularly for those that have imposed such taxes before."[9] That view was expressed in 2005, during a previous 'oil crisis' – when oil had risen to a mere $55 a barrel. The oil companies themselves say a windfall tax is bad news because it means they will be less able to extract oil from mature fields – a direct challenge to Gordon Brown's wish at the time of the Jeddah conference that part of the UK's response would be to push for increased extraction of the UK's jaded North Sea oil reserves. In response to the high prices, Al Gore asked a Washington DC audience in July, 2008 "Am I the only one who finds it strange that our government so often adopts a so-called solution that has absolutely nothing to do with the problem it's supposed to address? When people rightly complain about higher gasoline prices that are hurting our country, we propose to give more money to the oil companies and pretend that they're going to bring gasoline prices down? It will do nothing of the sort and everyone knows it."[10] This remark was given in the light of Presidential candidate Senator John McCain's pledge to open up new off shore oil fields and possibly Alaska's reserves too, but since Gordon Brown had appointed Gore as a climate change advisor, one hopes that the message might filter through. Gore's call is for policies that wean industrial economies off fossil fuels within ten years.

The variability in the price of oil, and predictions of reaching the peak oil tipping point have clearly not yet led to a political tipping point which could lead to a decisive shift from oil to renewable sources of energy, although as we have seen the oil crisis has given a spurt in that direction. Oil will be stretched as far it can be, and with the anticipated growth in the Chinese and Indian car markets, there will be little let-up in demand in a form of consumption for which there is still no credible energy alternative. The linkage of oil to renewable energy and nuclear power is a sleight of hand, which cannot do anything but harm either industry as it will be quickly found wanting if it raises expectations of early relief. Even the introduction of bio-fuels in line with EU targets (10% of road fuels to be bio-fuels by 2020) will do nothing to ameliorate the woes of motorists – these are, regardless of their currently questionable environmental credentials already referred to, not cheap. In the transport sector, the only rapid transition to a low carbon economy that would be effective and affordable would be massive modal shift, e.g. to mass transit systems, and by behavioural change, e.g. through greatly extended car sharing. Until electricity from renewable sources can be used effectively in vehicles there seems little hope that the bulk of our transport will be weaned off oil.

The aviation sector is even less likely to be weaned off oil anytime soon. Airline executives (with one or two notable exceptions such as Michael O'Leary of Ryanair) nevertheless talk up how much their industry is doing to curtail its GHG emissions to that extent that one might be forgiven for thinking that they're on the verge of cracking the problem. But the truth is very different. Whilst improvements in technology just as elsewhere in the economy can lead to reductions in GHG emissions per unit of activity – i.e. in the case of aviation, per passenger mile – if the number of passenger miles grows exponentially, then there is no overall reduction in emissions but a massive increase. The airports operator BAA for example, whilst not an airline reported that in 2007, 240 million passengers passed through UK airports, five million more than in 2006 and 81 million more than a decade previously.[11] It is easy to see how CO_2 efficiencies are swamped by passenger growth. Tyndall Centre, reporting research on behalf of Friends of the Earth concluded "if aviation growth continues, it could take up the entire emissions space for all sectors of the EU economy by 2040, and similarly for the UK by 2037, based on an atmospheric stabilisation target of 450 parts per million by volume. Moreover, between 2010 and 2020, UK and EU emissions could already be equivalent to their respective 2050 targets at the expense of other sectors."[12]

The aviation's industry's main plank in response to the growing concern over its CO_2 emissions has been to argue for inclusion in the EU ETS, and this is likely to happen in the third phase of the ETS beginning in 2012. So far as the aviation industry is concerned there are reasonable doubts as to what impact on its CO_2 emissions growth this step will have. If the intention is to curb aviation growth per se, then clearly the industry would not be so keen to join. Since the possible impact on fares is likely to be minimal, growth will probably continue although high oil prices may still be the main factor in that. The International Air Transport Association (IATA) projected possible additional costs associated with the ETS per ticket as €39.50 for a long-haul return flight or €9 for a short haul return flight.[13] But against that one has to consider the parallel EU policy of encouraging aviation growth, for example through the successful conclusion of talks to increase competition on transatlantic routes, leading to the 'Open Skies' agreement which could lead to over 500 extra transatlantic flights per month.[14] In other words, it is more likely that the inclusion of aviation in the EU ETS is only about offsetting its emissions and as Tyndall Centre said requiring other sectors to compensate by making ever deeper cuts – if they can.

In the early 2000s the aviation industry lobbied hard for inclusion in the EU ETS, as an alternative to taxation e.g. on their currently tax-free fuel (saving them around £9 billion per year) or the possibility of increases in other taxes such as the Air Passenger Duty (APD) . The airlines launched the 'Freedom to Fly Coalition' to fend off the growing environmental backlash against them, claiming not only that their carbon footprint was minimal but also, given Labour's strong majority in Parliament, appealing to legislators to remember how aviation should no longer be seen as a preserve of the privileged few, thus raising the spectre that if one was against the expansion of aviation one might also be anti-working class.[15] With trade unions backing the Freedom to Fly Coalition, it was a rare opportunity to see some unity in an industry which has been regularly torn apart by strikes and disputes often brought about by intransigent, private equity inspired managements. But with changes being proposed to the APD, the GMB union found itself in bed with some strange bedfellows, finding themselves in a "difficult position" agreeing with the likes of right-wing Tory MP Nicholas Winterton who had put down in the House of Commons an Early Day Motion (EDM) decrying the impact the new APD would have on UK jobs.[16] Rather than promoting job intensive and more environmentally friendly modes of travel like rail, the narrow sectoral approach to preserving jobs occasionally trumps the right thing to do.

Much to the aviation industry bosses' horror, things were changing in their entry terms to the EU ETS too. The industry had assumed that they would get all their carbon permits free of charge, as the power generation sector had received theirs in the first phase of the ETS – and which had permitted them to make massive windfall profits by passing on to consumers the extra cost associated with the presumed price of carbon permits. But now the principle of having to actually buy permits through auctioning has been introduced, British Airways Chief

Executive Willie Walsh was compelled to denounce politicians for their unprincipled, thoughtless behaviour:

> We have long advocated the inclusion of aviation in the European Union's trading scheme. This is now scheduled to occur from 2012. The final shape of the EU scheme is now becoming clear, following a series of discussions and parliamentary procedures over the last few weeks. I would be the first to say that I have serious reservations about some aspects of the scheme as it is now proposed. The original proposals have been made considerably more burdensome for airlines in financial terms by increasing the proportion of carbon allowances that are subject to auctioning, and imposing limits on what have been free baseline allowances for every other industry within the scheme. Auctioning is just another tax. Auctioning brings no direct environmental benefit whatsoever. It was not part of the original 'cap and trade' proposals, and seems to have been added to the package with little thought for its financial impact on airlines. I doubt whether any thought was given to its impact on airlines with oil at $150 a barrel.[17]

The upshot of this infamy would be clear, Walsh continued:

> If implemented as it now stands, without a global solution for aviation in place, the scheme will lead to a significant competitive disadvantage for EU airlines, resulting in a loss of jobs and reduction in services as international passengers bypass European hubs. It would be far better to implement this scheme initially for flights within the EU only, and to widen it to intercontinental flights when a global scheme that includes aviation is in place.[18]

The idea of transit passengers bypassing Europe would no doubt be very welcome to the millions of people living under their flightpaths, and the economic cost would certainly not be as great as aviation proponents suggest compared to the advantages, which might for example include being able to invest the billions necessary to build a third runway at Heathrow in something more useful, such as better rail links. As for Willie Walsh's appeal for a new global agreement we should not raise our hopes. The last comprehensive international treaty on aviation (the Chicago Convention) was sealed in 1944 and has been preserved by vested interests ever since.

In transport as in other sectors of the economy only effective carbon rationing offers the quick gains we need to tackle climate change. But in the absence of measures to radically alter our carbon intensive behaviour, the option which stands closest to delivery is clearly to be found in the renewable energy sector. The rapid introduction of renewable energy, such as wind, solar (in its several forms), wave, tidal, geothermal and biomass on both a large and small (microgeneration) scale is already a proven route in some countries and is growing faster as the threat of climate change sinks in. Efficiently harvested (e.g. coupled with complementary technologies like combined heat and power, CHP) one estimate of how abundant renewable energy is puts the worldwide supply of solar power at 10,000 times global electricity demand, or to put it another way, one 300 mile square of PV in the Sahara could easily supply all our electricity needs. In that last respect, proposals are already shaping up to harvest this actual infinite source (the Sun will last another nine billion years) of energy. But the introduction of renewable energy, particularly in the UK has been frought with problems.

On the 7th February 2007, a few weeks before the Budget, I was standing up and sitting down in my place in the chamber of the House of Commons, participating in the weekly ritual of trying to catch the Speaker's eye at Prime Minister's question time (PMQs). In truth I didn't have a question in mind, but was merely seeking to get my name on the Speaker's secretary's list of members who after a few attempts to be called at several PMQs might be more likely to be called at a later date. But he obliged me that day, and I clumsily cobbled together the following:

> In the light of the publication last Friday of the intergovernmental panel on climate change's fourth report on its assessment of climate change, which shows unequivocally that climate change is likely to be much worse than previously thought, does my right hon. Friend agree that we have to speed up the implementation of our policies and revise our targets, including that which might appear in the climate change bill? In the light of all that and of what he told the Liaison Committee yesterday, will he agree to meet me and representatives of the renewable energy industry to discuss the faster implementation of those policies?[19]

Asking 'will he have a meeting with me' at the end was a hasty afterthought, which was to have unintended consequences. Tony Blair replied:

> I certainly would be delighted to do that on behalf of my hon. Friend. This is an extremely important issue, and coming up in the next few weeks is an energy White Paper, which will address security of supply and the question of how we

replace the existing generation of nuclear power stations. Then there will be the climate change Bill, which, as my hon. Friend indicates, will make sure that we have sensible targets that this country can live with, and that we face up to our responsibilities in giving leadership on this issue. I point out that this country is one of the few in the world that will meet its Kyoto target; indeed, we will double it. We are leading the way internationally through the G8-plus-five dialogue, and making sure that we are working in harmony with our European partners and others to find a global framework that can allow us to put in place an international agreement to reduce carbon dioxide emissions after the Kyoto protocol expires.[20]

So the door was opened and after I convinced the Prime Minister's affable PPS Keith Hill that Blair had actually said yes to my request a meeting was set up a month or so later, for the Wednesday before Budget day. A small group of renewable energy representatives including Philip Wolfe of the Renewable Energy Association and Seb Berry of Solar Century met Blair in his room behind the Speaker's chair. Our allotted 15 minutes would flash past so I advised them to stick to a couple of major points, most importantly that the government's support mechanism for the installation of micro renewable generation was so small and so poorly structured that the monthly allocation of funds ran out by 11am on the first day of each month. It was an absurd situation – a pathetically small budget of only £12 million in the first place, divided up into smaller amounts each month, drip-fed at a painfully slow pace. Hardly indicative of government enthusiasm for microgeneration. Sitting comfortably on the sofas in Tony's Commons room and perhaps because Blair recognized Seb as an old acquaintance, the discussion was very amiable, whereas

I wasn't anticipating much enthusiasm on Blair's part – he was never into small renewables (or any renewables particularly) in the way that David Cameron claimed to be. Cameron was very publicly seeking to have a wind turbine installed on his London home's roof.

At the end of our short meeting, Blair said 'I'll have to speak to Gordon about this.' He was true to his word – the Budget announced an extra £6 million for microgeneration grants – a 50% increase. I thought that wasn't bad for 15 minutes' work tagged on to an afterthought to an almost accidental PMQ. But the satisfaction was not to last. Seb e-mailed me the day after the Budget to report that DTI (now DBERR) had suspended the whole microgeneration support scheme for a 'review.' It seems that the denizens of the DTI had taken offence that they themselves, having never pushed for this extra money were allowed to be taken by surprise. Their natural response was to seek to re-impose their authority by stopping the whole scheme. What I thought had been a good thing had turned into a fiasco, with microgeneration manufacturers and installers thrown into turmoil. When the scheme was eventually reinstated it had been so altered as to be worthless to most applicants. The size of individual grants had been reduced to the extent that the 'pay back' period for new installations would be lengthened considerably – so it simply wouldn't be financially worthwhile for most people to buy a renewable energy system for their home. Not surprisingly, the number of applications dropped off dramatically and the fund, rather than being oversubscribed became greatly undersubscribed. The extra £6 million would not be spent. The department had got its own back. The department's renewables recalcitrance didn't stop there. Late into 2008 it decided that applications for the greatly unspent

£50 million budget for Phase II of the Low Carbon Buildings Programme would have to be submitted by June, 2009, even though money does not have to be spent until March 2011.

These episodes - depressing though they are - are symptomatic of DTI/BERR's attitude to renewable energy, which despite ministerial rhetoric and the comparatively rare success nevertheless remains deeply hostile to an alternative which threatens the department's 'big box' mentality. This mindset is rooted in the glorious traditions of the department's past and shows an antipathy to solutions which are unorthodox. It means that what is unfamiliar – like power that comes from many smaller forms of generation, as opposed to the big nuclear, gas or coal powered plants – has a punishingly steep climb to prove itself. It is as if the government's long stated anti-interventionist pro-market philosophy of 'we don't choose winners' guarantees defeatist outcomes for new arrivals in the market place. This undoubtedly reflects the lobbying power of the existing big generators who are close to the department. Amongst them nuclear has been, and largely remains, wholly dependent on government finance for its survival but also reflects the fear in government that the issue of energy security, viz 'keeping the lights on,' necessitates a few big solutions rather than a more diffuse, decentralized approach. So although we may well keep the lights on with our familiar friends coal, gas and nuclear we will do little to stem our rising greenhouse gas emissions. We may even build new coal-powered electricity generation without carbon capture and storage.

Whilst my small contribution to the sad debacle of its microgeneration policy was indicative enough of BERR's antipathy towards renewable energy, a much bigger calamity was taking shape over the government's response to EU targets for renewables which came to light in the wake of the March 2007 EU Spring Ministerial Council. This proposed setting a new target of 20% of total energy demand across Europe, including transportation, to come from renewables. Reports at the time suggested that the UK went into those talks resisting setting a hard and fast target. This was indeed the case, as a leaked 'Ministerial Options' paper demonstrated.21 This paper was predicated on the premise that a strong emphasis on boosting renewable energy would depress the price of carbon and weaken the EU ETS. It opined "If the EU has a 20% GHG target for 2020, the GHG emissions savings achieved through the renewables target and energy efficiency measures risk making the EU ETS redundant and prices to collapse. Given that the EU ETS is the EU's main existing vehicle for delivering least cost reductions in GHG, and the basis on which the EU seeks to build a global carbon market to incentivise international action, this is a major risk." (emphasis added) So, it was not only the threat of renewable energy that DTI feared, but the unholy alliance of renewables and energy efficiency that could do so much damage to the ETS. It is worth digressing very slightly at this point to ask ourselves what is so special about the ETS that British interests might wish to delay progress even on energy efficiency.

In evidence to the House of Commons Public Accounts Committee in May 2004, Sir Brian Bender, the Permanent Secretary at Defra gave the game away (not that it was much of a secret) when asked by Brian Jenkins MP about the UK's own 'groundbreaking' emissions trading scheme which had commenced a couple of years prior to the EU ETS:

> *Mr Jenkins:* May I put it to you that the real priority here was to create a market and not to reduce emissions?

Sir Brian Bender: It was both but creating a market centre in
the City of London was a prize. Whether it is 50/50 or 60/40
I think it is impossible to answer but it was part of the prize
that the City would be the place, and we would look back to
the early 2000 years as a time when the decision had taken
place where this new commodity trading was centred in the
City of London."[22]

It should be borne in mind that at that time the three year
cost of the UK ETS, which involved fewer than three dozen
companies, cost the taxpayer £215 million, rather more than
the government's commitment to research and development
into renewable energy over the same period. The UK ETS made
a hotly disputed impact on GHG reductions, that is whether it
made any contribution at all over and above what the companies
which received the £215 million would have done anyway to
mitigate their carbon emissions. The UK ETS was essentially an
R&D scheme on behalf of the City, a business sector clearly in
need of more state aid than the tiny, hard pressed UK renewable
energy sector.

Another great theme of DTI's approach which bleeds through
the 'Options' paper but which is not stated in it, is that renewable
energy could threaten the relaunch of the nuclear dream. The
logic of this had to be stated by a Frenchman, Vincent de Rivaz,
the chief executive of the French state-owned nuclear generator
EDF who said "If you provide incentives for renewables . . .
that will displace the incentives built into the carbon market.
In effect, carbon gets cheaper. And if carbon gets cheaper, you
depress returns for all the other low carbon technologies [like
nuclear power]."[23] But de Rivaz seems profoundly confused, for
where his analysis of the intended role of the ETS falls short is

that it has so often been hailed as a mechanism for achieving precisely finding the cheapest (aka 'the most efficient') possible method of mitigating climate change.

Given that the DTI 'Options' paper was published four or five months after Sir Nicholas Stern had delivered his damming judgement on the markets' 'greatest failure,' i.e. climate change, and his assertion that markets alone would be insufficient to correct this failure, one could be forgiven for wondering whether DTI civil servants had actually read his report given their disdain for non-market solutions to climate change. Thus, with pained reluctance punctuating every step of their assessment of the potential British contribution to the EU 2020 renewable energy target, their paper asked ministers to "Agree that we should seek maximum flexibility in Commission proposal for directive to implement the renewables target." They recommended to ministers that "We signal to the Commission that although we have yet to commit to any particular approach, we are likely to look at least for options that retain flexibility to use non-EU energy investments to count towards the target."

Even though the 'Options' paper had been leaked by the summer of 2007 and dragged into disrepute the UK government's claims to be world leaders in actually fighting climate change, ministers pressed on with the paper's essential thrust. In March, 2008 the Guardian reported that 'in a speech that astonished European renewable energy companies, environment groups and other EU energy ministers,' BERR minister Lady (Shriti) Vadera said "It is imperative that cost efficiency is at the heart of our approach . . demand for renewable energy projects outside the EU should be considered [part of the renewable target]." This might, she suggested include carbon savings from coal-powered stations fitted with CCS.[24] It would be reasonable to assume she also included nuclear in this category. Thus, DTI/ BERR would have us believe that the EU target may not be merely an EU target, but might include anything that could save us a few bob and in the process would stunt our domestic effort – despite the fact that UK domestic per capita GHG emissions are higher than most. Such a policy may seem attractive to bean counters as opposed to carbon counters (and we'll return to the offsetting argument later) but completely ignores the damaging impact such an approach would have upon those EU countries, such as Germany, Spain and others which have chosen to invest heavily in new renewable energy sources and are now beginning to realise the rewards.

The assessment of the EU's 2020 targets in the 'Options' paper is quite clear: "The ambitious nature of the target itself means it lacks credibility – a recent gathering of financiers, to discuss the issue suggested that the target is unattainable, and business will need some convincing that it therefore will be strictly enforced and therefore provide much of [a] boost in EU investment." For financiers read 'City,' the same vested interest that Sir Brian Bender identified as being the beneficiary of a successful ETS. But the irony of the second part of the sentence quoted above cannot be missed: the renewables target has to be 'strictly enforced' whilst at the same time ministers are being urged to achieve maximum flexibility in achieving it. As the paper said "There are differences in the achievability of the target if it is defined as final energy consumption as opposed to primary consumption. This statistical interpretation can be used to make achievement of the target easier, regardless of whatever the final mechanism for the target's implementation is." So not only should we convince the Commission that foreign CCS and nuclear developments should be part of our 'flexible' approach, but we should also seek statistical tricks to fool people into believing we're achieving our targets – hardly a strategy for 'strictly enforcing' the renewable energy targets, and certainly not a strategy which would ensure the credibility of our achieving them.

This mealy-mouthed approach to the UK's participation in the EU 2020 targets was perhaps retired to the substitutes' bench by 2008, or at least one might be forgiven for thinking so when the government's renewable energy consultation was launched with a fanfare of publicity in June 2008. This seemed to signal that we had at last embraced the cause, with an eye-watering 'commitment' to spend £100 billion on renewable energy projects in just 12 years. It would be encouraging to hope that a major rethink had taken place, except as we have seen with Lady Shriti's comments in March 2008, the underlying 'flexibility' thrust still remained a year later, and in a July written ministerial statement on an informal EU Energy Council meeting on the 4th and 5th of July, Malcolm Wicks MP, the energy minister reported:

> During the debate on renewables there was a large degree of consensus on the importance of meeting the targets cost effectively. There was also widespread recognition that this can only be achieved with some level of exchange between member states allowing countries with potentially expensive domestic renewables resource to buy more cheaply elsewhere in the EU. There was general agreement among ministers that a UK/Germany/Poland proposal for a system of exchange between the member states represented a promising way forward."[25]

It is curious that the point about 'exchange' has to be repeated in such a short paragraph – nothing here about how the

UK intends to spend £100 billion developing its domestic renewables resource, which given that it is one of the best available resources in Europe might be classed as potentially the least expensive to harness. Or might the plan be that a good part of that £100 billion should be foreign investment coming through a 'flexible mechanism?' But if that were to be the intention then somebody else, elsewhere in the EU would be claiming the credit for carbon dioxide emission reductions made in the UK. The 'exchange' only helps us meet our GHG reductions if we're paying for them ourselves.

In the foreword of BERR's renewable energy consultation, John Hutton, the former BERR Secretary of State said that "The UK's proposed share would be to achieve 15% of the UK's energy from renewables. That is almost a ten-fold increase in renewable energy consumption from where we are now. It will involve all of us in a revolution in how we use and generate energy."[26] As we can now see, the commitment should not be taken at face value, since the government seeks to achieve some of the target abroad, although quite how much of the 15% will be sought overseas is not yet clear. The confusion persists throughout the document. We are told for example that "increased investment in renewables in the UK to meet a 15% energy target in 2020 will reduce UK gas imports by 11-14% in 2020" – which might be true if we were talking about a 15% reduction in UK energy consumption – but we are not.

Nor indeed is the government's proposal for a 15% contribution from renewables particularly ambitious by EU standards, since out of 27 member states, our target is in the bottom bracket of EU states – along with smaller countries like Cyprus, Luxembourg, Hungary, Malta and The Netherlands. At the time of the publication of the consultation document, the UK was third from bottom in what renewable energy we had actually developed: 1.5% over Luxembourg's 0.9% and Malta's 0.0%

Against this backdrop, the civil servants in 1 Victoria Street (BERR's HQ) are right to be nervous about the credibility of our plans to meet the EU 2020 target. We are still lurching along from one policy extreme to another, clutching our comfort blankets of 'clean' coal and nuclear, whilst undermining any progress towards a sustainable energy supply with what can only be seen as a fantasy vision for renewable energy. There is no evidence whatsoever that the government intends to achieve the levels of renewable energy investment to turn that vision into a reality. We should remind ourselves that it took the government 15 months from the initial EU council meeting in March 2007 just to get to the point where it felt able to launch a consultation document; the consultation continued until September, 2008 and the results are to be published in 'Spring' 2009, by which time two years will have elapsed – and by which time of course the UK will be on full general election alert and any hope of certainty for investors will be put on hold whilst the outcome of that is awaited. Should the party of government change then the funding mechanisms may change too. Thus it could be wishful thinking to imagine that any real progress on this 'revolution on how we use and generate energy' will begin much before 2010. Investors will wonder whether or not a new government would wish to consult further on a new strategy which it could call its own?

Contrast the British approach to that of the German government, which under both Chancellors Gerhardt Schroeder and Angela Merkel has been far more focused. During Schroeder's time in office, the Bundestag in 2000 passed the Renewable Energy Sources Act (EEG). In that year the share of renewables in total primary energy consumption was 2.6%, and had doubled by 2006. In terms of the share of renewable energy in gross electricity consumption, the respective figures were 6.3% and 11.6% A figure above 13% is forecast for 2007 – which if it was achieved means that the target set in the 2000 Act for 2010 will have been achieved three years early.[27]

A statutory report to the Bundestag in 2007 on the implementation of the EEG is worth quoting at length:

> The Renewable Energy Sources Act continues to generate considerable impetus for innovation, domestic value added and employment. According to a recent analysis, domestic turnover from the installation and operation of renewable energy systems increased from €18.1 billion in 2005 to around €22.9 billion in 2006, with around €14.2 billion of this being directly attributable to the Renewable Sources Energy Act. Exports will become increasingly important in future: in 2006, for example, the export share of the German wind energy sector was already above 70%, while that of the photovoltaics sector was around 30%. This has been accompanied by a substantial increase in employment in the renewables industry. The number of people employed in all the renewable energy sectors rose from 160,000 in 2004 to around 236,000 in 2006. Around 134,000 of these jobs, i.e. almost 60%, were created as a result of the Renewable Energy Sources Act.[28]

Of course, this is not achieved without cost, and the modelling of the German government reports that if one takes into account reduced German consumer spending power on other goods and services (because they're being forced to spend more on energy) then the net impact on employment is still a growth in jobs of up to 78,000 by 2006. It is the cost of the EEG that makes British policy makers so nervous, and they despair that the German renewable funding mechanism – the feed-in tariff – is more market interventionist then the British model, which was largely inherited from the Thatcher era. To the latter charge one might retort that it bloody well needs to be, if we want to tackle climate change but to the former charge, the German Environment Minister Sigmar Gabriel noted that the differential (i.e. additional) costs of EEG power were €3.2 billion in 2006 and said "That's a euro per month per household. And I think that's a damn cheap gig" – not least since the policy had also led to the avoidance of more than 100 million tonnes of CO_2 emissions per year. Further research also showed that German renewables had had a dampening effect on the electricity market price, saving consumers €5 billion – outweighing the differential costs added by the EEG.[29]

As an opening hand for the EU's Spring Council meeting in March 2007 therefore, Germany came with a success story – but contrasting their subsequent response to that meeting with the UK's response is revealing. We have already seen how the UK has earned the title 'Renewables Laggard of the EU,'[30] and as the UK locked itself in a padded cell and threw away the key, the German government stepped up its whole game. By August 2007, at a specially convened weekend Cabinet meeting an Integrated Climate and Energy Action Plan (the Meseberg Package) was launched, which announced 29 new measures to tackle climate change, including agreement to set a new GHG reduction target of 40% by 2020 compared to 1990. They summed it up thus "With Meseberg we are moving away from the attitude in international climate policy of 'your first' towards 'this is what I'm doing, what about you?'

Leading by example is the only way to break the deadlock in international negotiations."[31]

Clearly the German government's enthusiasm for renewables is heavily based on its environmental strategy, but as references to employment growth show, there is a clear industrial strategy in mind too. Matthias Machnig, a German environment minister, talking to a meeting in the UK parliament said that it was not Germany's average 960 hours of sunshine that inspired a decision to invest in photovoltaics – but the desire to get ahead in R&D, export opportunities and employment growth.[32] He believes that with such policies in renewable energy up to 500,000 jobs may be created. By contrast BERR's vision, outlined in its consultation document anticipates up to 160,000 new jobs – hardly enough, if this were just one measure of how to justifiably claim leadership on tackling climate change.

Perhaps the biggest bone of contention with UK policy – a bone dug up over and over again by a small handful of UK MPs who follow ministers' every attempt to bury it – is the way in which renewable energy is financed. The method chosen by most EU member states is the feed-in tariff, which pays a guaranteed price for every KWh produced from a renewable energy source. The guarantee lasts for 20 years, and as the installation matures, the price degresses, i.e. as the energy source becomes financially more profitable, the subsidy decreases. Different rates of feed-in tariff apply to different sources of energy dependent on how mature their respective technologies are. Another key feature that has helped the feed-in tariff to become Europe's most successful system of financial support for renewables is guaranteed, priority access to the grid. Thus potential electricity generators of whatever size know that access will not be denied them either by deliberate obstruction or by – as is more likely to be the case in the UK – obstruction by bureaucratic complexity. The UK system, known as the Renewable Obligation, sets a national target for how much renewable energy should be supplied to the grid in any one period, and then leaves the market to decide how to meet that target – and failure to meet the target results in a penalty or 'buy-out' payment having to be made. In other words, it is possible not to meet the target and claim the system is still working. Depending on the availability of Renewable Obligation Certificates (ROCs) – which reflects the success or otherwise of reaching targets – their price may go up or down, adding considerable uncertainty into the market. On top of that generators seek out the cheapest way to achieve their targets, so whilst onshore wind farms have been the most popular route, other technologies have been neglected. Because of the market uncertainties about prices for renewable energy, investment is less likely to be risked by small investors and many observers – including this one – believe that the RO is much preferred by large electricity generators, since it helps preserve their market share by discouraging new competitors. In Germany by contrast many smaller generators have flooded into the market for power, from individuals and communities through to municipal authorities. Innovation and technological adaptation are more likely to be the fruits, as environment minister Machnig believes it will be.

Many of the large electricity generators also have an interest in the renaissance of nuclear power, and as we have seen in the comments from EDF's chief executive Vincent de Rivaz, these giant corporations remain ambivalent towards renewable energy. They still argue most strongly for their historic energy base which remains, still, their largest source of revenue – and subsidy.[33] Will these corporations be enthusiastic partners

in overcoming the 'severe practical difficulties' which led –
reportedly – to BERR seeking as late as October 2007 to resile
from the proposed renewable targets?[34]

Suppliers will no doubt take their cue from the consultation
paper, which reveals the lack of confidence the government has
in its own Damascene conversion:

> This document contains a range of possible additional
> measures to encourage deployment of renewable energy in
> the UK. These measures are designed to achieve a 15% energy
> target of the UK by 2020. However in a market economy policy
> alone cannot guarantee outcomes. How much these measures
> will deliver will depend on how energy companies, developers
> and investors in the market, and the supply chains which serve
> them, will respond to the signals we provide. It will also depend
> on how successful we are in overcoming the constraints on
> development. Indeed, because renewable deployment depends
> on decisions by governments, businesses, communities and
> individuals in all parts of the UK, it will depend to some extent
> on how committed we are as a society to achieving our goals.
> (emphasis added)[35]

In other words, do this minister and you'll be out on your ear: the
electorate won't have it, either because of the cost or nimbyism.
So let's just see how impossibly difficult it will be before we
revert to Plan B, which is what we always wanted: more coal
and nuclear. If with existing measures, encouragements, signals
and of course the ever cost-effective market we still cannot
as things stand expect to get much beyond 5% of renewable
energy harnessed by 2010 (the government's target was 10% by
then) what may we ask has changed?

The lack of ambition, as opposed to soundbite opportunism and the grudging acknowledgement of EU targets reflects the fear of taking on a burden rather than seeking an opportunity. If the EU had a plan to ensure that 100% of our energy should be sourced from fossil fuels and nuclear, it is doubtful whether anyone in BERR would see that as a challenge – after all, these are the forms of power generation which already receive the most subsidy. It is the way in which the renewable energy proposition is posed which causes it so many problems. Imagine an analogy with the development of the railway network. If railways had been presented as a means of overcoming Britain's 'chronic social mobility problem' of the 1830s (not that people thought they had such a problem necessarily) then it would have caused all sorts of angst as to quite how much should be spent on tackling it, and perhaps complex financial mechanisms would have been created to deal with it – perhaps with 10, 20 and 30 year targets to meet. As it was a problem that had not yet been defined found a solution, one of the many consequences of the railway 'manias' that overtook Victorian society.

The first of these manias, dating from 1844 provides a peacetime example how quickly a society cold be transformed by investment in new technology – and, as it happened in the absence of public subsidy. Christian Wolmar, in his absorbing history of British railways Fire and Steam, wrote

> The real rush started in the autumn of 1844, the deadline for tabling Bills to be considered in the next parliamentary session. Whereas forty-eight Acts had been passed in 1844, 240 Bills were presented to Parliament in 1845 (of which precisely half were sanctioned), representing 2,820 miles, a doubling of the existing network. Had all these railways been built, the capital

required – about £100 million – represented more than one and a half times the country's gross national product of £59m for that year. There is no equivalent in modern times of such a major investment scheme accounting for so much of a country's economic activity, but perhaps the closest comparison would be the allocation of resources to Britain's defence during the Second World War.[36]

This achievement was delivered with a much smaller government, with less planning, regulation and all the other bureaucratic hurdles that we have today, but that is not a sufficient reason to explain the comparatively unfettered nature of the first railway mania. More it was a question of investors seeing the returns that could be made and leaping on to the bandwagon. Inevitably, some of the bandwagons proved to be duds and there were plenty of unprofitable lines. Indeed, there was much opposition too, eerily equivalent to modern-day nimbyism. Landowners had to be bought off. Some objections were reminiscent of today's often eccentric opposition to wind farms. One landowner protested that if 'this sort of thing is permitted to go on, you will in a very few years destroy the noblesse.'[37] The noblesse perhaps envisaged themselves as part of Britain's natural landscape to be protected at all costs, but 150 years later very few would argue that Britain's railway heritage is not a much loved part of the British landscape. By 1847, in just four years, the total authorised track mileage had reached 9,500 which if it all had been built would have cost £250m to build, equivalent to well over £19bn today.[38] Within a few years, two thirds of these lines were built. At such short notice one wonders where all the engineers, surveyors, technicians, drivers, guards, signallers and porters came from? Prior to the first mania, the industry showed all the signs of idling in the doldrums, developing somewhat fitfully.

We should ask why we cannot have a renewable energy 'mania' today – looking at the whole gamut of 20-odd renewable energy sources, not just wind. Clearly this calls for a root and branch review of the potential resource and the financial and technological means of harnessing it. Has the government laid the foundations for this in its Renewables Strategy, presented for consultation in July, 2008? Has there really been a sea-change in a government department of which it was revealed in August, 2008 had failed to spend any of its budget for the 'Wave and Tidal-stream Energy Demonstration Scheme,' worth £42million since 2004?[39] It seems only fair on past experience to think not and the ball was back in BERR's court to prove otherwise.

Thankfully in the autumn of 2008, in a long overdue move which saw government responsibilities for energy supply and demand brought together under one roof in the Department of Energy and Climate Change, it appears that some of the lessons of past failures were beginning to be taken on board. DECC's Secretary of State, Ed Miliband, in his first front rank post has brought a new sense of engagement with the joined-at-the-hip issues of energy and climate change, and soon after his appointment improvement were made to the Energy and Climate Change Bills then completing their final stages in Parliament. There was of course the previously touted increase in the UK's long-term greenhouse gas reduction target, from 60% to 80%; but there was also movement towards the more successful German feed-in tariff method of supporting renewable energy. When the government had at first reluctantly accepted that this would be a good idea, at least for microgenerated electricity, it proposed a maximum capacity of 50Kw – just about enough for one house. Miliband saw off vehement opposition from the major electricity utilities, and moved the maximum up to 5Mw – a 100-fold increase. Bearing in mind that an average power station is rated at 1Gw, it is nevertheless important to keep even this improvement in perspective.

Notes

1. Speech to Alliance for Climate Protection, Washington DC 17th July 2008
2. Speech to the C40 Large Cities Summit, New York, 15th May 2007
3. An approach which seems popular with voters – see "US voters back offshore oil drilling" in the *Wall Street Journal Europe*, 22nd August 2008 for example.
4. A comment made in a meeting between the author and Nick Thomas, UK Public Relations Director of ExxonMobil in 2004
5. Comment made at the launch of the 41st BP Statistical Review, 11th June 2008, 1 St James's Square, London
6. And new for old in other areas does not always mean less energy is consumed. Flat screen televisions consume more power than their cathode ray tube predecessors on a size for size basis, but of course because the bulk of a flat screen TV is smaller than CRT, consumers want bigger screens, once again forcing up electricity consumption.
7. http://www.publications.parliament.uk/pa/cm200304/cmselect/cmenvaud/490/4033003.htm
8. *Financial Times*, 13th June 2008
9. *Financial Times*, 31st October 2005
10. Al Gore, speech to Alliance for Climate Protection, op cit
11. BAA Corporate Responsibility Report, 2007
12. *Growth scenarios for EU and UK aviation, contradictions with climate policy*, FoE at www.foe.co.uk/resource/reports/aviation_tyndall_research.pdf)
13. *Guardian*, 9th July 2008
14. *Independent*, 1st March 2008
15. This appeal to working class solidarity of course is bedevilled by the airlines own determination to put extraordinary efforts into winning high value passengers, with special treatment for those who fly 100,000s of miles each year, or with the establishment of business class only airlines such as the ill-fated Silverjet airline.
16. GMB letter to Labour MPs 27th June 2008
17. Speech to SBAC event, Farnborough Air Show, 16th July 2008 at: http://www.sbac.co.uk/pages/92567080.asp
18. *ibid*
19. Hansard, 7th February 2007 col. 834
20. *ibid*
21. *Draft Options Paper on Renewables Target*, c. March, 2007, DTI, leaked to and in possession of the author.
22. *The UK Emissions Trading Scheme: a new way to combat climate change*, 46th report of session 2003-04, Public Accounts Committee, p. Ev 9.
23. *Guardian* 29th March 2008
24. *ibid*
25. Written Ministerial Statement, House of Commons, 10th July 2008
26. *UK Renewable Energy Strategy*, Consultation BERR, June 2008 p.1
27. *Renewable Energy Sources Act (EEG) Progress Report 2007*, Federal Ministry for the Environment, Nature Conservation and Nuclear Safety.
28. *ibid*
29. *new Energy*, Berlin, issue four 2007 p.16. Thankfully the battle for a less market orientated approach and a greater role for planning has been joined by the European Parliament, whose

Committee on Industry, Research and Energy has sought to alter the EU Commission's proposal for a thoroughly market-led renewable energy directive to something more sensible. For example contrast the following two sections, the first original proposal and the second as amended by the Committee:

(h) "support scheme" means a scheme, originating from a *market* intervention by a *Member State, that helps* energy from renewable sources *to find a market by reducing the cost of production of this energy, increasing the price at which it can be sold, or increasing, by means of a renewable energy obligation or otherwise, the volume of such energy purchased.*

(h) "support scheme" means a scheme, originating from a *policy* intervention *through which incentives for the expansion and increased use of* energy from renewable sources *are created or strengthened. National support schemes include in particular renewable energy obligations, investment aid, tax exemptions or tax breaks, tax refunds and direct price support schemes, especially feed-in and premium schemes.*

From DRAFT REPORT, on the proposal for a directive of the European Parliament and of the Council on the promotion of the use of energy from renewable sources (COM(2008)0019 – C6-0046/2008 – 2008/0016(COD))
Committee on Industry, Research and Energy, Rapporteur: Claude Turmes, European Parliament.

30. Renewable Energy Association Briefing no. 3, 2007
31. Statement of Federal Ministry for the Environment, Nature Conservation and Nuclear safety, December 2007
32. Speech to the All Party Parliamentary Climate Change Group, House of Commons, 18th June 2008
33. Subsidies to coal, oil and gas and nuclear have always exceeded those for renewables, e.g. a European Environment Agency report showed that in 2001 in the EU-15 coal took €13bn, oil and gas took €8.7bn, nuclear got €2.2bn and renewables got €5.3bn. EEA Briefing 2/2004 Copenhagen.
34. '"The commission, some member states and the European parliament will not want the target to be diluted, though others may be allies for change" another leaked BERR advice note chirped' – *Guardian*, 23rd October 2007
35. BERR renewable strategy consultation, op cit p.6
36. ChristianWolmar, *Fire and Steam: A New History of the Railways in Britain*, Atlantic Books, London, 2007 p.88
37. *ibid*, p.63
38. calculated at www.measuringworth.com
39. *Guardian*, 6th August 2008

5

pile 'em high and sell 'em cheap: the great nuclear delusion

> *Nuclear cannot actually deliver the climate or the security benefits claimed for it. It's unrelated to oil. And it's grossly uneconomic, which means the nuclear revival that we often hear about is not actually happening. It's a very carefully fabricated illusion. And the reason it isn't happening is there are no buyers. That is, Wall Street is not putting a penny of private capital into the industry, despite 100-plus percent subsidies.*
>
> Amory Lovins, Chairman, Rocky Mountain Institute[1]

A crucial part of tackling climate change means weaning ourselves off fossil fuels which release enormous amounts of greenhouse gases into the atmosphere and investing in new, zero or low carbon renewable energy sources. In the UK, the move to such energy supplies has always been a fitful process bedevilled by government indecision and U-turns. By 2008 it was still not clear whether this pattern could be changed, but at the start of the year a great and unfulfilled dream from the past had been revived.

The nuclear power industry had miserably failed to live up to Margaret Thatcher's ambitions for it in the 1980s and by the time the Hammer Of The Coal Miners left office in 1990 nuclear power had entered into a near terminal, 25-year decline. She had wanted to see 10 new nuclear power stations built, but only one – Sizewell B – was constructed. Calamities elsewhere in the world, from Three Mile Island in the United States to Chernobyl in the Soviet Union led public opinion away from nuclear. Countries such as Sweden and Germany decided against building any new nuclear power stations and pledged to let their existing fleet run its due course and not be replaced. In the UK, with the privatisation of electricity generation, nuclear's fate received another blow. As former Energy Secretary and then Chancellor Nigel Lawson put it "Had it not been for privatisation, who knows how much longer the country would have been paying the price of the phoney economics of nuclear power."[2] Nuclear power's economics became even worse when the so-called 'dash for gas' in the 1990s replaced much coal-powered electricity generation and led to lower prices. By the early 2000s, it seemed as if the final nail in the coffin had been hammered in when the No 10 Downing Street Policy Innovation Unit (PIU) published a report which suggested that nuclear may never again be an option for electricity generation – the emphasis now would be on renewable energy. Patricia Hewitt, the Blairite Trade and Industry Secretary even went so far as to say that 'a major new nuclear programme would have undermined the drive for efficiency and renewables' although she told the BBC "We are not absolutely ruling out new nuclear build forever."[3]

That was in 2003, when the government published an Energy White Paper following up the PIU report. But the nuclear industry had begun to rouse itself from its creeping rigormortis, and for the next three years commenced a major lobbying exercise to recover its self-declared role as the 'energy of the future.' Redoubtable proponents of nuclear power like energy minister Brian Wilson led a more sophisticated approach to the problem of restoring nuclear's fortunes. This was to be a twin tracked strategy of proclaiming both nuclear and renewable energy as natural bedfellows in the search for a low-carbon energy supply. Wilson was undoubtedly committed to both, and went so far as being one of the first to have a Windsave micro wind turbine attached to his Scottish home, a photograph of which adorned Windsave's leaflets for years afterwards. Intensive lobbying, always conducted against a background when it was always going to be hard to believe that a pro-nuclear Prime Minister like Tony Blair would really ditch nuclear power eventually hit its target, and by 2008 a new pro-nuclear Energy White Paper was published. This followed a consultation on nuclear power which many considered fatally flawed, but which the government obviously hoped would deliver the coup de grace to nuclear's opponents, who for a long time had been able to claim the support of a majority of public opinion. The Nuclear Consultation Working Group convened by Dr Paul Dorfman at Warwick University concluded "the key assumptions underpinning the government's approach to the nuclear consultation remain open to critical analysis. We are profoundly concerned that these assumptions have framed the questions asked by the government during the nuclear energy consultation, and were designed to provide particular and limited answers – and those answers risk locking in UK energy futures to an inflexible and vulnerable pathway that will prove unsustainable."[4] The government's nuclear 'consultation' exercise was successfully challenged and overturned in the courts, all to no avail – there would be no stopping nuclear, no further pause for reflection.

How hollow the consultation was is shown by evidence of the nuclear power industry's embeddedness in government thinking well before the consultation began. One small example of this could be found in the Draft Magnox Decision Document, which had originally been prepared in 2001 and was circulating for final approval in 2005. The document gave a detailed assessment of the clean-up of the soon to be made redundant Magnox nuclear power stations and was published by Defra on the basis of advice from the Environment Agency. On page 48 the document stated "The Ministers are satisfied . . . that nuclear power is consistent with the objectives of sustainable development from a viewpoint of resource availability, economics, reduced environmental and intergenerational equity, and the detriment to future generations from the operation of nuclear power stations is likely to be small." Since this statement certainly conflicted with the PIU report and subsequent government statements, the Environment Agency was challenged to explain it. Sir John Harman, chair of the Environment Agency was equally concerned and wrote "I agree with your concern about paragraph 155 of the document, which purportedly quotes an Environment Agency statement. In fact, it is a gross misinterpretation of our position. The quotation is from BNFL's applications for authorisation of the Magnox power stations, which we included in our decision document. We have already forcefully pointed this out to Defra. They have apologised to us and agreed to issue a correction to the document as quickly as possible to all consultees."[5] Reputations were at stake. On page 33 the Magnox document said "Ministers . . are satisfied that the Agency is independent of the nuclear industry."

But Defra and the EA are only responsible for cleaning up the mess left after the nuclear horse has bolted. Of the commissioners of the beast - the DTI itself - Jeremy Leggett, a former member of the government's Renewable Advisory Board had this to say: "I have heard two of Tony Blair's senior colleagues confirm that the DTI has long suppressed renewables to make space for nuclear. The slow-motion UK treatment of renewables during the last five years, while renewables markets abroad have grown explosively, now makes a sickening kind of sense."[6]

Patricia Hewitt's doubts – if they ever really existed – were eventually replaced by the almost devil-may-care nuclear enthusiasm of John Hutton. There could be little surprise that the new Secretary of State would be an enthusiast – he has represented a 'nuclear' constituency Barrow in Furness, the home of BAE Systems and the Trident nuclear submarine shipyard since 1992. Something of a one-horse town, Barrow also served as a port for nuclear shipments to and from nearby Sellafield. It would be suicidal for an MP representing a seat without a gold plated majority to speak out against the nuclear interest, and clearly Gordon Brown's choice of Hutton to be Secretary of State for the energy department of BERR in June, 2007 must have had only one outcome in mind.

On the 10th January, 2008 Hutton rose from the government frontbench to make his statement on the new Energy White Paper. My response was:

> We have to be honest and recognise that the statement is as full of holes as the Sellafield reprocessing plant. Margaret Thatcher promised 10 new nuclear power plants and delivered one. We have heard about the Finnish experience and know that Germany, which is tackling climate change with a thorough

energy policy, is eradicating the possibility of new nuclear plants there. When does my right hon. Friend anticipate that the first new nuclear plants will be commissioned and how many will we get?

Mr. Hutton: As I tried to say in my statement, I am not going to set a limit or attempt to calculate the number; that is not for Ministers to do in an energy market that operates on liberal parameters. Industry estimates suggest that the first such nuclear power station could be operational in the UK by 2017. I think that an optimistic assessment, but it is what the industry is saying.[7]

By this time it had become clear that opponents of nuclear had become a tiresome, ideologically driven rump in the government's eyes. The 'usual suspects,' a small group of Labour backbench nuclear opponents including Malcolm Meacher, Des Turner, David Chaytor, Joan Walley, Alan Whitehead and Alan Simpson would be portrayed as being slightly obsessed if not loopy whereas pro-nuclear MPs, especially if they had nuclear constituencies would be patted on the head, showered with kind remarks and admired for their long-sighted wisdom.[8] The problem for nuclear power's parliamentary opponents was that no matter how much the subject might be debated, there was no need for new legislation to be enacted to permit new nuclear power stations being built. Thus, there would be no substantive vote on the issue. Even if there was, there would be little chance of success for nuclear power's opponents given that the Conservatives, with some minor reservations, had welcomed Hutton's statement. The same coalition that had brought us the Iraq War would sustain new nuclear build, predicated on equally dodgy premises.

Given the grandiose claims made by the nuclear lobby on behalf of nuclear power's low carbon qualities – an argument which may well have won many doubters over to its standpoint – it is essential to examine these claims in more detail. Bearing in mind the injunction of the IPCC that we must peak and then commence the reduction of greenhouse gas emissions by 2015, it is clear that the urgency of the task grows with every passing day. It is also clear that new nuclear build has two key milestones to pass before it could make a contribution to the task of reducing greenhouse gas emissions. The first of these is that it merely has to replace our existing fleet of nuclear power stations. This provides around 18% of UK electricity supply. Until new build can achieve this replacement, there will by definition be no replacement by nuclear of fossil fuel generated electricity.

Once that milestone is passed, then new nuclear build has some chance of making a contribution to reducing carbon emissions. Since the government itself had made so much of the argument that nuclear power would help combat climate change, one might be forgiven for thinking that it would know when the fulfillment of this most urgent of tasks might be accomplished. As the following written parliamentary question and answer illustrates, nothing could be further from the truth:

> *Colin Challen:* To ask the Secretary of State for Business, Enterprise and Regulatory Reform what assessment he has made of the timescale for new nuclear power stations to produce more electricity than is currently produced by existing nuclear power stations.
>
> *Malcolm Wicks:* We are not setting a target, or a limit, to the amount of electricity to be generated in the future by new nuclear power stations.[9]

Quite apart from the fact that the answer bears no relationship to the question, the embedded answer is 'we don't know.' The reason we don't know, of course is that the government's non-interventionist stance in the energy marketplace means that by definition it cannot know what nuclear power's contribution is likely to be. In effect, we have abdicated our responsibility to combating climate change, if electricity generation has anything to do with that, and are more prepared to fiddle around the edges, as is illustrated in other chapters. Perhaps there is a comprehension problem about nuclear. Speaking to oil industry representatives in Banchory, near Aberdeen in May, 2008, Gordon Brown said: "We want to do more to diversify our supply of energy and that's why I think we are pretty clear that we will have to do more than simply replace existing nuclear capability in Britain . . We will be more ambitious for our plans for nuclear in the future." Given the audience, and the way the media spun this comment – in the midst of an oil supply crunch – Brown appeared to be telling the British public that nuclear was the solution to our oil-related woes. In which case, he couldn't have been more poorly informed, either on the timing of the delivery of additional nuclear, or what the electricity it generates is likely to be used for, almost certainly not transport which is Britain's overwhelming use for oil.[10]

What reasonable supposition can be made about when nuclear power might make a significant contribution to reducing greenhouse gases? In the course of his statement and in the answer above John Hutton alluded to 2017 as being the first possible date a new nuclear power station could come on stream. That's if everything works to plan, with streamlined planning and licensing and no contractors' building hiccups to slow things down. In a later answer, he spoke of 2020 as being a realistic date – for the first new nuclear power station to be commissioned.

Experience might teach us that things in the nuclear world rarely go according to plan. Not only in the UK back in the period of the first nuclear building mania but today too, in modern Europe there is ample evidence that wishful thinking has been a guiding spirit for the advocates of nuclear energy. The first of only two new European nuclear power stations being constructed at present is in Finland and that deserves a closer look.

In early 2005 permission was given by the Finnish government for work to commence on the construction of the Olkiluoto 3 nuclear power station. This will be Finland's fifth nuclear power station, and the first to be built since 1982. The background to the Finnish development provides us with some insight into the inflated claims of the nuclear power industry. The Finns have knowledge, they are not a backward, Johnny-come-lately set-up, their development is being led by the most experienced nuclear power station builders in the world – the French.[11]

The demand for electricity in Finland is growing sharply. In 1970, the supply of electricity stood at around 23 TWh; by 2004 this had risen to around 80 TWh. In recent years, according to a presentation given to the author by the Finnish Radiation and Nuclear Safety Authority in 2005, the increase in power supply had been met as follows:

Source	% increase	% current share
Biomass	19.9	13
Russian gas	19.9	12
Nuclear plant uprating	19.3	25
Coal and oil	14.9	20
Peat	9.9	7
Wind	0.6	0.1
Electricity import (Nordic hydro and Russian nuclear generated electricity)	15.5	23

It is anticipated that power consumption will rise by 2020 to reach 103.3 TWh, leaving a predicted shortfall in generating capacity of 7,000MW. Clearly, without greater efforts to reduce demand or increase supply, the shortfall would create serious problems.

A proposal by the government in 1991 to build a new nuclear reactor was defeated in the Finnish Parliament in September, 1993. Parliament by statute must have the final say on whether to approve a 'decision in principle' to build, unlike in the UK. At the core of the decision the concept of whether it would be for the "overall good of society" has to be considered. Neither a majority of MPs nor public opinion believed it was, and it was thought at the time that energy savings potential and increased use of gas and renewable energy would meet projected demand.

What changed? According to Green MP Oras Tynkkynen, three factors influenced public opinion:

Firstly, climate change. The increasing public awareness of global warming and its potential impacts on Finland has grown considerably in recent years. Both the nuclear industry and the then government were able to use this argument to sway public opinion.

Secondly, waste disposal. The nuclear industry was able to claim that they had found a solution to this problem, with deep burial in stable bedrock.

Thirdly, the Russian 'problem.' This can be defined in two ways. One is the diminishing memory of Chernobyl, the other is a fear of an increased dependence on Russian energy resources. As we have seen above, Finland has met some of its increased demand for power supply from both Russian gas and nuclear generated electricity. Culture and history combine to make further reliance on this source suspect. There is, for example, an ongoing debate in Finland as to whether she should join NATO.[12]

Climate change is an issue which the nuclear industry has made much of, the arguments are well rehearsed and I do not intend to dwell on them here. The security of supply issue in relation to Russia is also familiar, indeed similar concerns arise in the UK, particularly as regards the 'gas from Gazakstan' syndrome (referring to the energy-rich but somewhat politically unstable regimes of central Asia).

What is of particular interest is how the Finns dealt with the nuclear waste issue. This was done prior to any further decision being made on whether to build any more generating capacity. Given Finland's existing nuclear power structure, the issue of waste already posed a problem. In 1983, the government agreed a spent fuel management policy which decided that the selection of the site for disposal must be made by 2000 and construction should start by 2010 to become operative in 2020. It was also agreed that only nuclear waste created in Finland could be stored in Finland, and that no nuclear waste created in Finland could be disposed of anywhere else but Finland.

In May, 2001 Parliament agreed that final disposal could take place, and that the site would be at the existing Okliluoto nuclear power station. It was agreed that the waste should be 'disposed of safely using proven technology; that it should not be a burden to future generations and that the management of it should not have to rely on foreign support.' As we shall see, it can be argued that at least two of these principles may not be honoured. Future liability and foreign support are both contentious. The problem can be exemplified in how the current new build proposals are to be financed.

The new power station is to be financed entirely from private funds, with decommissioning and waste disposal costs fully incorporated into the price. Various bodies have taken shares in the project, and will receive their return in electricity supplied to them from the new power station. The shareholders include energy intensive business users such as steel, paper and pulp industries. Other shareholders include public authorities. For example, Helsinki City Council has taken an 8% share. The projected lifespan of the power station is 60 years.

Two questions arise over the financing: the original build costs, and the long term future of the waste. The consortium which won the contract, TVO, is made up of German Framatome ANP GmbH, French Framatome ANP SAS and Siemens AG. There have been claims that the construction finance package has broken EU state aid rules and a legal challenge has been taken before the EU Court of Justice. The allegation appears to be that consortium members have created a deal which has wrongly absorbed or suppressed true costs in order to win the contract.

The long term waste disposal costs must be calculated over a period of many centuries, at the very least. It is hard to see how this could be otherwise, given the life span of high level nuclear waste. To get some measure of what is being considered (for what is by any standards a modest nuclear programme serving a country with a population of only 5.2 million people) the official publication Nuclear Energy in Finland gives a good impression:

"During their 50 to 60 years of operation, the present Olkiluoto and Loviisa nuclear power units produce some 3,650 tonnes of spent fuel for final disposal. The spent fuel arising from the Olkiluoto 3 unit during its 60 years operation lifespan is estimated to be about 2,200 tonnes."[13]

This spent fuel is to be buried in a complex of tunnels in deep bedrock between 420 and 520 metres underground, requiring the excavation of some 330,000 m3 of rock. After the spent fuel canisters have been buried in their own special chambers, these will be back-filled and sealed off. But the plan nevertheless remains that they should be retrievable. According to Nuclear Energy in Finland, "The possibility of retrieving the spent fuel is demanded in the Finnish Government's decision."

Thus 'final disposal' means final disposal with fingers crossed. What should happen if the waste had to be retrieved? Who picks up the bill? The costs of building the new nuclear plant also includes some protection against terrorism. The Olkiluoto 3 plant's core will be passively protected by an inner one metre thick concrete encasement, and a further two metre thick wall. There is no suggestion that Finland's existing nuclear power plants will be so protected, indeed this seems to be something of a design impossibility. The protection offered by the new concrete structures seems to have been tested only by impact testing with steel balls.[14]

Clearly there are a range of uncertainties in the foregoing which must have an impact on costings – and who pays for the worst case scenario. This is clearly a question for any new nuclear build proposal.

As we have seen, Finnish power consumption is predicted to rise to 103 TWh by 2020 from around 80 TWh in 2004. Although the proposal for a new nuclear power station was launched in 1998, it is not now anticipated that Olkiluoto 3 will be commissioned until 2011 at the earliest, and that is already nearly two years later than planned. Thus it can be seen that for a period of well over ten years it will have done nothing to alleviate Finland's energy supply problem. Whilst it is recognised that Finland is not well endowed with marine or wind renewable energy sources, it is hard to believe that the increase in the use of wind from the above figures is all that could be achieved. It is also the case that Finland has an estimated 60 billion trees, so biomass could have a greater potential than its current 13% share.

Finland is working on a new national Climate Change and Energy Strategy which may address how to make more use of renewable energy as well as how to make better use of energy. But there are also strong suggestions that a sixth and even a seventh nuclear power station should be built. This being so, it is hard to see renewables making a significantly larger contribution to Finland's energy needs, even if they have the capacity to do so.

If Finland's pro-nuclear decision were to be cited as a positive precedent for the UK, the following questions would need to be satisfactorily answered:

1. Will any new nuclear build proposal be fully privately funded, with the price to include all decommissioning and waste disposal costs, and in the case of the latter, in perpetuity?
2. Will the waste disposal issue be fully resolved prior to any further discussion of new-build?
3. Will the UK handle only its own waste problem, i.e. not to export or import waste for disposal?
4. Given the UK's considerable potential as a terrorist target, will protective measures be more extensive than Finland's passive systems? Who will pay for these?
5. Will the UK's extensive renewable resources be sidelined?[15]
6. Will the UK Parliament be allowed to decide the issue of whether new nuclear build is for 'the overall good of society?'

The last of these questions has never been asked in the UK – the focus has largely been on questions dealing with the technical aspects of nuclear power, not least the expense and the disposal of radio-active waste. So the answer is 'no' – a predetermined consultation exercise was deemed sufficient.

Since construction work began on the Olkiluoto plant, the projected completion date of 2009 has been put back several times, and as we have seen it is now expected to be commissioned in 2011, two years behind schedule. Estimates vary but the cost has also risen – from £2.2 billion to around £3 billion. Very much on the basis of experience in Finland, Dr Wulf Bernotat, Chairman and Chief Executive of E-on has suggested that the UK government's assessment of costs, made in the 2008 Energy White Paper of £2.8 billion per power station would probably be closer to €5 or 6 billion.[16] many of the problems which have delayed the building of the new Olkiluoto power station have been blamed on the inadequate training and skills of the construction workers, leading to 1,400 safety notices being issued. With only two nuclear plants being built in all of Europe (the other is at Flamanville in France), this lack of skills could be the resurgent nuclear industry's biggest stumbling block, and belies the confidence of the UK government that, in the words of former energy Secretary of State John Hutton 'local skill shortages could be made up from abroad.'[17]

Alongside the government's inability or refusal to state what proportion of our future energy needs may be supplied by nuclear lies an equal inability of the industry itself to come forward with a consistent plan. Perhaps there is some desperation all round not to make predictions, given the nuclear industry's exceptionally bad record in delivering anything on time and on budget. The biggest players cannot agree what they are capable of. In a letter to MPs in January 2008, the chief executive of EDF, the French state subsidised electricity generator said "EDF is committed to building the urgently needed new capacity. Contingent on the government's decision we have been working for nearly two years on plans to build, by 2017, the first of up to four new nuclear power plants in the UK, using EPR [European Pressurised Reactor] technology."[18] However, rivals E-on UK said in a memorandum to the House of Commons Environmental Audit Committee in May 2008 that "no more than one or two plants are likely to be in operation by 2020 and none by 2015."[19]

As mentioned above one way in which the government has tried to spin new nuclear power is its supposed environmental benefits. These have been presented as chiefly low carbon but also as almost a renewable source of energy itself. There are important reasons why the industry would wish to be classed as both, since it needs to attract the finance and support that is available to low carbon or renewable energy sources, created by mechanisms such as the European Union's Emissions Trading Scheme (EU ETS), the UK Renewable Obligation (RO) or the UN Clean Development Mechanism (CDM, administered by the UNFCCC). Even if the public might be willing to give its approval to new nuclear – to keep the lights on – it doesn't seem very happy to see nuclear receive yet more public subsidy. But wherever the money comes from to pay the inevitable subsidy it will always at the end of the day come from the consumer's pocket.

Nevertheless, to avoid the word subsidy or at least the appearance of it (the government has said many times that it will not brook any public subsidy of new nuclear) ways will nevertheless have to be found to subsidise it. One argument then is that it should be treated as a renewable form energy.

One government minister took a brave stab at making this case in 2005[20]

> The Parliamentary Under-Secretary of State, Department of Trade and Industry (Lord Sainsbury of Turville): My Lords, the Government recognise that nuclear power shares many of the same environmental benefits as renewable energy, particularly with regard to greenhouse gas emissions. The technical question of whether nuclear energy is or is not a renewable source of energy turns on how one defines "a renewable source of energy", and the view one takes on the supply of uranium, the use of other materials and the commercial prospects of nuclear fusion.[21]

Many proponents of nuclear power believe that theirs is an industry that has been unfairly excluded from the Labour government's fiscal incentives designed to reduce our dependence on fossil fuels - precisely because they believe nuclear "shares many of the same environmental benefits as renewable energy." In doing so they perhaps forget the huge sums that flowed their way through the creation of the Non Fossil Fuel Obligation (NFFO) in the 1980s. There is also a view that perhaps 'renewable' and 'reprocessing' have similar connotations; or that there is a near limitless supply of uranium available to meet our burgeoning demand for energy. The question of uranium supply is significant since the discussion about uranium has moved on to similar territory that oil now occupies, with much debate revolving around when oil will reach its 'peak' or 'topping' point. The uranium 'topping point' (when reserves fail to keep up with demand) may not be far off.

Estimates of how large uranium reserves are depend not merely on absolute quantifications of the presence of uranium, but also on the economics of extracting it. The second of these assessments must be explored not only in terms of financial cost, but also in the amount of energy required to extract and process uranium into a usable fuel and the amount of CO_2 and other greenhouse gases which will be emitted in the process. The first question – what is the absolute quantity of uranium – is therefore better stated as the quantity of uranium available to us within reasonable parameters. The financial benchmark widely used in industry is that estimates of deposits available at maximum production costs of around US$80 per kg U provide for worldwide reserves of just over 3.5mt.[22] If the price is raised considerably to US$130 per kg U around a further .5mt will be available – a law of diminishing returns.[23] The European Commission on the other hand have stated reserves at a much lower figure of 2mt.[24]

If measured only in financial terms any definition of uranium reserves is bound to be elastic. At the World Nuclear Association's (WNA) annual conference in London in September 2005, a presentation on the WNA's Market Report said: "fuel supply is potentially short beyond 2015, unless the lower demand scenario occurs . . future uranium supply is now a big issue. Actually the uranium market has been concerned about it for some time and accordingly, the price has been increasing the last couple of years."[25] Clearly, if all the predictions about growing nuclear demand come true, e.g. that China is seeking to increase nuclear generating capacity from 6.5gW today to 40gW by 2020[26] regardless of the law of diminishing returns already noted, then it will perhaps become economic to consider nuclear reserves above the 4mt level – but

as we shall see this will present new problems. It is instructive
to note that there is much confusion in the process of estimating
reserves – a report by the British Nuclear Energy Society speaks
optimistically of an "Independent assessment [which] puts the
total scale of conventional uranium resources of around 11mt,
enough to last for around 170 years at current consumption
rates . . This would be enough to provide for a lifetime's fuel for
all of today's nuclear reactors worldwide, plus all those which
might be built as far ahead as 2050, even in a scenario where
world nuclear capacity were to triple to 1200gW by that date."[27]
Such an optimistic view needs to be taken with a pinch of salt,
as nuclear analyst Paul Mobbs notes:

> Primary uranium currently supplies around half the world's
> 64,000 tonnes/year demand, with the other half coming from
> ex-military uranium stocks. If we take global reserves at four
> million tonnes, this gives a resource lifetime of 62.5 years. [If
> on the basis of a fivefold expansion of the nuclear industry]...
> demand would rise to 320,000 tonnes, and the lifetime of the
> resource reduces to 12.5 years.[28]

This is a critical assessment but still appears more generous
than that of the WNA above, and illustrates the difficulty in
trying to pin down the size of cost-effective reserves. But with a
history of wildly inaccurate forecasts, the nuclear industry itself
seems the last place to go in search of the truth.

The energy costs – and thus CO_2 emissions – of extraction
place absolute limits on worthwhile quality nuclear deposits.
There is little point extracting uranium if it takes more energy
to get it out of the ground than it will deliver as a fuel. If we
take life cycle analysis (LCA) CO_2 emissions as a rough proxy

for energy input, the nuclear option appears to have a clear advantage over fossil fuel alternatives – always provided that the original uranium source is classed as 'rich'. Industry claims that nuclear's LCA CO_2 emissions amount to just $4gCO_2$ per kWh are common. This compares with $8gCO_2$/kWh for wind power, 430gCO2/kWh for gas and $955gCO_2$/kWh for coal.[29] But once again, the estimates the industry make are all over the place. The IAEA in 2000 produced a report which showed that wind had around a third of the 'Greenhouse Gas Emissions from Power Production Chains' of nuclear.[30] No doubt there are differences in the way that such figures are compiled – e.g. whether all greenhouse gases are counted or just CO_2 – but nevertheless all such reports scotch the idea that nuclear is a 'carbon free' option. Indeed, nuclear may not even be that much better than gas – WWF found that there was, depending on the source of information, "a whole range of figures for nuclear's LCA from $34gCO_2$/kWh to $230gCO_2$/kWh."[31]

A reliable and even less rosy assessment of the CO_2 costs of nuclear power has been made by independent analysts Jan Willem Storm van Leeuwen and Philip Smith. Their extensive study of the literature shows that

> if rich, 'soft' ores are available (i.e.[with a uranium mass] equal to 1% or higher), the nuclear power plant succeeds after about two full-load years [in producing less CO_2] than a gas-fired plant. If the ores are leaner, say 0.1%, this takes about nine years. For poorer ores (i.e. ore grades lower than 0.01%) the nuclear plant would be responsible for more CO_2 emissions than if the same amount of (electrical) energy were to have been obtained from burning the fossil fuels directly.[32]

Some proponents of nuclear power suggest that we need just one more generation of nuclear to get us over the 'generation gap' and to give us time to develop other technologies which will ensure we meet our carbon reduction targets. This option, as suggested by Professor Sir David King, would involve the use of plutonium currently held in storage, and which he says would have to be disposed of whether or not that process were to generate electricity.[33] This is another aspect of the 'nuclear is renewable' proposition which posits that we would effectively be making good use of something which otherwise would have to be treated as waste. An attraction of this idea is that because the safe disposal of plutonium has a fairly high financial cost in any case, the extra cost of using it as a fuel would be marginal – superficially altering the economics radically in its favour. It has also been argued in the past that if used in breeder reactors, the use of plutonium would lead to the creation of new nuclear fuel – a 'genuine' case of being renewable. But the experience with breeder reactors is of a technology which has met with overwhelming technical problems, and could not be of any use in a medium to long term timescale. The reactor models currently touted as being ready for short term development do not include breeder designs.

A 'halfway house' appears to exist with mixed oxide fuels – MOX. This combination of uranium and plutonium, which uses reprocessed spent fuel as well as plutonium from former military stocks, appears to offer a recycling opportunity for uranium and thus an extended nuclear life warranty. MOX is anticipated to rise in use from around 30 reactors today to over 70 – up to 20% of the world's reactors – by 2010.[34] Such reactors all need to be specially designed and where necessary existing plant adapted to take MOX. Two problems have bedevilled MOX – cost and safety. The UK's reprocessing facilities at Sellafield have never proven economic, and a history of falsified safety analyses led in 1999 to a shipment of the fuel to Japan having to be returned. It is also alleged that the manufacture of MOX leads to much greater radioactive discharges, and the Irish government supported by the Norwegian government have strenuously opposed the Sellafield operation. Reprocessing can prolong the life of uranium as an energy source, but it has considerably greater financial, safety, proliferation and environmental costs. For these reasons, Mohamed ElBaradei, Director General of the IAEA said "We should consider limitations on the production of nuclear material through processing and enrichment, possibly by bringing these operations exclusively under multilateral control, while guaranteeing the supply of fuel to legitimate users."[35] Is this something which can be contemplated in the near future? It seems highly unlikely.

So is nuclear renewable? The answer must be a resounding 'no.' A cursory examination of the evidence provides no other answer. The very suggestion illustrates how desperate nuclear proponents are in seeking to convince us that they have a viable solution to the challenge of climate change.

As we have seen in this section, nuclear power's low carbon credentials can be challenged. With a global renaissance in nuclear power leading to a massive expansion in demand for uranium, there will inevitably be a price to pay. To deny that would be fatuous, but since we live in a world where old habits die hard, we must expect fatuousness. Estimates vary, but on the industry's most ambitious scenario we could see the development of 1,000 new nuclear power stations, bringing the total up to 1,400. This seems over the top – constraints in engineering skills and materials are likely to act as a significant brake on new nuclear development. But everybody it seems wants new nuclear. The case of Iran is notorious, of course, with doubts about Iran's long term peaceful intentions – but fears have been raised about Syrian plans too, and Egypt is considering new nuclear along with other Middle Eastern states. France has held bilateral negotiations with Algeria, Jordon, Libya, Morocco, Tunisia and the United Emirates, locations which have led some wags to label such proposed civilian nuclear plant 'pre-deployed nuclear weapons.'[36] Venezuela is also interested in pursuing nuclear power, and is interested in deal with both Argentina and Iran "to advance in new areas such as nuclear and atomic energy" according to Rafael Ramirez, their energy minister. Naturally such a move would not be welcome in the United States.[37]   The International Atomic Energy Agency (IAEA) believes much of Africa will one day want their fair share of nuclear power. Such developments may not be motivated by the desire to reduce global warming, but more a desire to join the nuclear club, with all the horrendous connotations that holds.

In Indonesia, one of the world's largest coal exporters and users with rapidly rising carbon emissions also arising from deforestation, plans for new nuclear will do little to alleviate greenhouse gas emissions. Speaking at a meeting at the 2007 Bali UNFCCC conference, Dr Hudi Hastowo, from the Indonesian National Nuclear Energy Agency (BATAN) told the audience that Indonesia had commenced a nuclear programme which he claimed would deliver its first power station in 2017. Yet he presented a slide which showed that whilst nuclear would contribute just 4% of electricity by then, there would be a much bigger demand for coal (up 16% from 42% to 58%), and more gas (19% to 27%) whilst hydro would fall from 9% to 4% and geothermal would reduce from 5% to 4%. In other words, at great expense Indonesia would not even replace its planned reduction in renewables with nuclear, never mind tackle the growth in the use of fossil fuels. True, there was to be a marked reduction in oil, but this would be more than offset by the take-up of coal.

The Bali IAEA meeting also heard more about – in former Chancellor of the Exchequer Nigel Lawson's words – the 'phoney' economics of nuclear. Bert Metz, from the IPCC produced figures which showed that pricing carbon at $50 a tonne would encourage just 2% more nuclear generation by 2030 – up to 18% of world electricity generation. Dr Ferenc Toth from the IAEA told his audience that "Nuclear always takes longer than you expect" and went on to give eleven reasons why we should actually regard nuclear power as a highly unpredictable part of the energy mix:

1. Nuclear power was hit by economic restructuring
2. Nuclear power was hit by increased energy efficiency after the oil shocks of the 1970s
3. Nuclear power was hit by slower demand
4. Nuclear power was hit by excess capacity
5. Nuclear power was hit by energy market liberalisation and privatisation
6. Nuclear power was hit by the oil price collapse
7. Nuclear power was hit by a surge in gas supplies
8. Nuclear power was hit by the Three Mile Island episode
9. Nuclear power was hit by high interest rates
10. Nulcear power was hit by the Chernobyl explosion
11. Nuclear power was hit by the break-up of the Soviet Union

It is hard to see nuclear power as anything other than a Cinderella, for whom every circumstance has to be just right before it can work. But Dr Toth might also have mentioned another factor which explains the decline of interest in civil nuclear power, namely the easing of international relations after the end of the Cold War and the consequent 'peace dividend' which removed some of the interest in maintaining large nuclear weapon arsenals. The economics of the first generation of civil nuclear power stations was inextricably linked to the development of nuclear weapons. Given the preponderance of economic reasons explaining the spluttering death of nuclear power, Tony Blair was wise to get elected in 1997 on an anti-nuclear platform, as the Labour Party manifesto made clear:

> Effective environmental management is an increasingly important component of modern business practice. We support a major push to promote energy conservation - particularly by the promotion of home energy efficiency schemes, linked to our environment taskforce for the under-25s. We are committed to an energy policy designed to promote cleaner, more efficient energy use and production, including a new and strong drive to develop renewable energy sources such as solar and wind energy, and combined heat and power. We see no economic case for the building of any new nuclear power stations.[38]

Interestingly, the party's 1997 general election policy guide went one step further and said "Labour sees no economic or energy case for the building of new nuclear power stations." (emphasis added)[39] Unfortunately, DTI dragged its feet, or worse on the manifesto's positive pledges, thereby undermining the government's room for manoeuvre in honouring its non-nuclear pledge.

So when the 2008 Energy White Paper relaunching Britain's civil nuclear power industry was revealed there was, naturally much celebration within the industry. But there was also some relief for opponents too, since it was their belief that there was not sufficient support in the White Paper to actually get any new nuclear power stations off the ground. Nuclear power does not exist anywhere in the world without subsidy, either directly from the taxpayer through taxation, or from the consumer through higher prices. As has been suggested above, one way the nuclear industry would wish to achieve viability is, in the words of EDF's Vincent de Rivaz "a robust long term carbon signal."[40] When asked by this recipient of Mr Rivaz's letter to explain what he meant by "the right framework for investment" no reply was forthcoming. Would it require more or less than the $50 per tonne of carbon remarked upon by the IAEA? Given nuclear power's consistent cost overruns, we should expect it to want a higher price – but this would confound the logic of the ETS, which we have often been told is the best way to deliver carbon reductions because it seeks out the least costly ways of doing so. How will other sectors react to a carbon price which has to be inflated to allow nuclear power to operate? And if a high carbon price is thought necessary, why not introduce it to bring on the faster adoption of zero carbon technologies, which bring earlier bonuses in delivering carbon emission reductions?

Carbon reductions could in any case be made at a much lower cost than with a new programme of nuclear power, as Professor Kevin Anderson, of the Tyndall Centre for Climate Change Research has pointed out: "We could very easily compensate for [a short-term growth in carbon emissions from increased fossil fuels use] with moderate increases in energy efficiency. If you've got money to spend on tackling climate change then you don't spend it on supply. You spend it on reducing demand."[41]

Another problem with the economics of nuclear power, which works decisively against new nuclear generation, is its opportunity cost. This is the cost of lost opportunities. One such loss, as hinted at above by Kevin Anderson, is a lack of impetus when it comes to introducing energy efficiency. Nuclear power is posed as a solution to global increasing energy demand – in this sense it is proposed as a business-as-usual solution, and the message that that sends out is that more electricity can be obtained, relatively speaking at the flick of a switch. One cannot easily dismiss the government orchestrated demonstrations in Tehran where the demonstrators carried identical placards declaring that 'nuclear power is our obvious right.' It is hard to see any government anywhere orchestrating demonstrations calling for energy efficiency as a right, but those that support the development of nuclear power often use arguments which lean towards the Iranian proposition. Consumption one feels always has the upper hand over efficiency.

Other nuclear opportunity costs emerge which also ought to be factored into the equation. Amory Lovins of the Rocky Mountain Institute has convincingly demonstrated how the economics of nuclear power do not compete with those of renewable energy. His detailed analysis led him to the conclusion that:

> . . these competing technologies not only are being deployed an order of magnitude faster than nuclear power, but ultimately can become bigger. In the U.S., for example, full deployment of these very cost-effective competitors (conservatively excluding all renewables except windpower, and all cogeneration that uses fresh fuel rather than recovered waste heat) could provide

~13-15 times nuclear power's current 20% share of electric generation-all without significant land-use, reliability, or other constraints. The claim that "we need all energy options" has no analytic basis and is clearly not true: nor can we afford all options. In practice, keeping nuclear alive means diverting private and public investment from the cheaper market winners-cogeneration, renewables and efficiency-to the costlier market loser.[42]

Perhaps, as the recent experience of T. Boone Pickens, the legendary Texan oil billionaire who is investing $2 billion in giant new windfarms in Texas shows, there are big opportunities to be had in the U.S., which with its much larger and less densely populated land mass may be thought more financially and politically viable for renewable energy than here in the U.K. But this assessment is easily challenged. Work by the Green Alliance back in 2005 compared new nuclear power with the potential micro-renewable power only, and found that this highly decentralised approach meant that "an investment of around £13 billion in three micro-generation technologies – considerably less than that needed for new nuclear plant – would provide around 15GW additional capacity," easily on a par of the new capacity that could be bought if the same sum was spent on new nuclear.[43]

There is a conflict between nuclear and renewable energy – those who insist there is not are deluding themselves, or are being deluded by the nuclear industry's new-found but wafer-thin enthusiasm for the alternative. At least some in the nuclear power industry are willing to be frank in their assessment of this conflict. Vincent de Rivaz, Chief Executive of EDF said: "If you provide incentives for renewables ... that will displace the incentives built into the carbon market. In effect, carbon gets cheaper. And if carbon gets cheaper, you depress the returns for all the other low-carbon technologies [like nuclear power]."[44]

This self-serving logic comes as no surprise, the only surprise is that as yet Whitehall has not yet learnt quite how master this brand of chutzpah. In reality, we would love to be as single-minded as the French, who generate four fifths of the electricity from nuclear, but we don't want to admit that they have achieved what they have with a) a state-driven generating sector and b) without the assistance of our much vaunted liberalised energy markets. A side-effect of our confusion has delivered the ownership of nearly every UK utility and energy technology sector into foreign hands. The only British owned company thinking of bidding to build nuclear reactors for our new fleet of nuclear power stations is, ironically, BAE Systems, with many years experience building our nuclear submarines – in John Hutton's constituency of Barrow in Furness.

The political narrative of UK energy policy is based on a strong institutional culture which harbours a deep suspicion of anything which began life as 'alternative' and which has by definition a small political constituency. Big problems need big solutions, so the old, familiar 'big box' generator has a head start in the corridors of power. Quite how big the big box 'solution' might turn out to be is a matter for conjecture, but it will be comforting to all who admire this approach that some in the nuclear industry see a "trajectory for a 21st century nuclear industry that achieves the deployment of nothing less than 8,000-10,000 Gigawatts of nuclear power - a twenty fold increase. Such growth is scientifically and commercially feasible, and to plan for anything less would be to invite environmental disaster."[45]

A debate has opened up about nuclear's climate change-specific green credentials, but should anyone argue that it offers hope or even that it doesn't matter one way or the other, they are making a huge mistake. In the short period we have to reduce our GHG emissions, a medium term 'solution' like nuclear power is of no more use to the passengers on the Titanic than a salvage ship arriving three weeks later.

Notes

1. Amory Lovins, *Nuclear Power: economics and climate-protection potential*, Rocky Mountain Institute 2006 www.rmi.org/sitepages/pid171.php#E05-14)
2. Nigel Lawson, *The View From No. 11* Bantam Press, London 1992 p.170
3. http://news.bbc.co.uk/1/hi/sci/tech/2793855.stm
4. (Quoted in *RENEW* 171 stop press, Network for Alternative Technology and Technology Assessment (NATTA), Open University, January 2007. The nuclear power industry's public relations drive included a dubious advertisement which proclaimed "Decommissioning Berkeley showed that one new [sic] British business has a clear future." This showed three photographs of the Berkeley nuclear power station, the last of which was simply a green field where it once stood. Of course, no green field exists – it is merely a doctored photograph. Indeed, it is unlikely that any nuclear power station site will ever end up once again as a green field, not merely because of the technical issues of removing every last remnant, but also because such sites will be required for the next generation of nuclear power stations. Complaints were made by the author to the Advertising Standards Authority (ASA), but were rejected. It turned out that the ASA had 'pre-approved' the advertisements on behalf of British Nuclear Group, rather negating the point of making a complaint to them in the first place.
5. Letter to the author dated 14th November 2005
6. Quoted in the *Guardian*, 3rd January 2007 and Renew, op cit
7. *Hansard*, 10th January 2008 Col. 534
8. More than just kind words – a good dollop of public money too, especially for any constituency that chooses to accept nuclear waste, which the Times reported may be in line for a £750million cash 'inducement.'
9. *Hansard*, 21st April 2008 : Col. 1766W
10. http://news.bbc.co.uk/1/hi/uk_politics/7424158.stm
11. This section is based on interviews with Professor Jukka Laaksonen, Director General of Finland's Radiation and Nuclear Safety Authority (STUK), Riku Hittunen, Head of Energy Administration and Nuclear Energy Division, Ministry of Trade and Industry, and Orsa Tynkkynen MP held 14th October 2005; and *Nuclear Energy in Finland*, Ministry of Trade and Industry, Helsinki, July 2005
12. *ibid*
13. *Nuclear Energy in Finland, op cit*
14. It may be more prudent to test the safety of the cores with something a little more serious, such as a rocket propelled grenade. The RPG 29 can penetrate 30 inches of steel. RPGs have been used against British Army Challenger 2 tanks by Iraqi insurgents. The tanks' explosive reactive armour has been found unable to resist the latest RPG technology. See *DailyTelegraph*, 12th May 2007
15. One of the fears proponents of renewable energy have is that nuclear energy will force out investment in renewables. This is an understandable fear, and is based on hard evidence. Nuclear power has always taken the lion's share of R & D expenditure. Even in the later years of the development of nuclear power in the 1970s and 1980s, UK R & D investment

regularly exceeded $1 billion – whilst renewable energy R & D languished in the low tens of millions. Whilst nuclear R & D spend dropped dramatically in the late 1990s onwards, it was not compensated for with an equivalent investment in renewables – or indeed any other form of energy. See Council for Science and Technology, *An Electricity Supply Strategy for the UK*, May 2005

16. *Times*, 5th May 2008

17. *Guardian* 28th June 2008

18. Letter to MPs dated 23rd January 2008

19. Memorandum to Environmental Audit Committee, May 2008

20. This section first appeared in *What's in the Mix: The Future of Energy Policy*, SERA, London 2006

21. House of Lords *Hansard*, 22nd November 2005, Col. 1498

22. RWE Aktiengesellschaft, World Energy Report 2005, Determinants of Energy Prices, Essen 2005

23. Paul Mobbs, Mobbs' Environmental Investigations, written evidence to House of Commons Environmental Audit Committee (EAC), September, 2005

24. Energy Green Paper, Towards a European Strategy for the Security of Energy Supply, European Commission, 2001, quoted in Mobbs, *op cit*

25. Quoted in EAC memorandum to members, November 2005

26. RWE *op cit* p.43

27. British Nuclear Energy Society, evidence to EAC September 2005

28. Mobbs, *op cit*

29. Nuclear Industry Association, quoting 1999 DTI commissioned report, evidence to EAC October 2005

30. Institute of Mechanical Engineers, evidence to EAC September 2005

31. WWF-UK evidence to EAC September 2005

32. www.oprit.rug.nl/deenen/

33. Oral evidence to EAC 17th November 2005

34. Nuclear Issues Briefing Paper 42 Mixed Oxide Fuel (MOX), Uranium Information Centre Ltd, July 2003   www.uic.com.au/nip42.htm

35. *New Scientist*, p.17 10th July 2004

36. *Bulletin of the Atomic Scientists*, 3rd June 2008

37. http://www.foreignpolicy.com/story/cms.php?story_id=3987

38. *New Labour Because Britain Deserves Better*, Labour Party 1997

39. *New Labour, new life for Britain*, Labour Party, 1997

40. Letter to MPs, dated 23rd January 2008

41. *Guardian*, 17th January 2006

42. Lovins, op cit

43. Rebecca Willis, *Small or Atomic? Comparing the finances of nuclear and micro-generated energy*, Green Alliance, London, 2005. The Green Alliance paper's conclusions are not exceptional: the Oko-Institut e.V. in Darmstadt, Germany drew similar conclusions about the poor financial performance of nuclear. See their Comparison of *Greenhouse-Gas Emissions and Abatement Cost of Nuclear and Alternative Energy Options from a Life Cycle Perspective* published in 2006 which said "that renewable and DSM options (including gas-fired co-generation with combined cycles) are more competitive in terms of GHG abatement costs, even if no external cost value is allocated to the risks of nuclear electricity."

44. http://www.guardian.co.uk/environment/2008/mar/29/renewableenergy.climatechange?gusrc=rss&feed=networkfront

45. *The Necessity of Nuclear Power: A Global Human and Environmental Imperative*, John B Ritch, Director General of the World Nuclear Association.

6

don't frighten the horses

On currency. Yesterday is a spent cheque. Tomorrow is an IOU. Today is the only cash you have. Spend it well. Make the most of now.

Vodafone advertisement[1]

Oh yeah? The thoughtfulness that underpinned our most recent consumer boom was captured in Vodafone's sentiment 'Make the most of now.' Not only must we live for the present, but we could borrow from tomorrow too (after we'd spent our cash wisely of course – only then start on the plastic). 'Spending today' responsibly meant that Dave (aka Dave J. G. O'Reilly) could reassuringly tell us (his wisdom was revealed in double page newspaper spreads) from his desk as CEO of the Chevron Corporation that "Energy will be one of the defining issues of this century."[2] A short homily on how Chevron would spend tomorrow's IOU followed. A little later BP, which had been reincarnated briefly as 'Beyond Petroleum' was asking "What on earth is a carbon footprint?" With self-deprecating abandon they told us that "Everybody in the world has one."[3] Of course, all sorts of innovations were in place to reassure us that all was being done to lessen any anxiety these discoveries may cause. In complete harmony with Dave and BP was the announcement by Boeing under the heading "Partnership is discovery" that with their partners they were "developing an electric motor-driven airplane powered by fuel cells. Eventually fuel cells may replace existing auxiliary power units, which could benefit the environment. Just another stop on the journey to discovery." (emphasis added)[4] On the road to discovery? But surely not to the copywriters' court of truthfulness - are we meant to believe that auxiliary power units will give us 'an electric motor-driven airplane? Because they certainly didn't mean auxiliary aircraft engines.

The carbon pukers' spokespeople's romantic imaginings know no bounds, and no green claim can be left uncapped no matter how absurd. Lexus couldn't contain themselves. "The Lexus RX 400H is a luxury car with a conscience. A luxury car that's better for the environment but without the compromise, thanks to our unique Lexus Hybrid Drive technology . . So if you want to make a stand for the planet, but arrive in style, find out more by visiting your local Lexus Centre." The RX400H's carbon emissions are only 192g/km, that is a mere 62g – or one third – over the limit the EU is seeking to impose in order to achieve CO_2 reduction targets which are still not ambitious enough.[5]

Test drive it today. And take some glossy leaflets home, where you can digest them over a glass of wine in the garden, under an 'alfresco appliance.' But: please follow the "simple guidance to help you ensure an alfresco lifestyle whilst at the same time, taking care of the wider environment." The manufacturer's advice somewhat tediously means having to turn down your interior heating whilst you are outside; sitting close to the appliance (unlike the loafers photographed in the manufacturer's leaflet); wearing sensible outdoor clothing (the featured loafers are not complying again) and most woefully of all turning your patio heater off "if the weather warms up."[6] Thankfully, patio heaters have lost favour in some quarters and not least with B&Q, who after initial resistance have stopped restocking this most abject of all 'lifestyle' items. But as one lifestyle item dies, another takes its place and perhaps the most ubiquitous of these is the flat screen telly, a must-have for any self-respecting consumer regardless of the serviceability of their previous cathode ray tube model. A warning has come rather too late that these wonderfully savvy replacements may have "a greater impact on global warming than the world's largest coal-fired power stations."[7] And that's just a reference to GHG releases made in their manufacturing process, never mind the extra power required to keep an inevitably larger stock of new flat screen TVs switched on. The stresses of coping with these multiple threats to the environment can only lead to one conclusion: get away from it all. Since the 1990s the cruise business has grown as never before, and thankfully since aviation and maritime GHG emissions are exempted from the Kyoto Protocol they won't count towards our official UK CO_2 targets. How about a flying, sailing, train riding "Cairo to the Cape" once in a lifetime escape, visiting Zimbabwe and other African countries for a mere £15,995 (including an optional 'gorilla tracking experience')?[8] And wouldn't it be good to pay a little extra to relax with our primitive primate cousins - whose only carbon footprint is their flatulence - and see what can be learnt from them? (The lesson being that they don't care about the environment either, they're just animals.) Of course, arguments are made that 'eco-tourism' is good for developing world economies, but since the growth in aviation by 2030 could account for half of our CO_2 emissions, isn't it time to take a more intelligent approach?

Advertising is core to consumerism since it encourages our wants, our desire to feel good. With very little amendment, it can also tell us how what we want may also address our concern for the planet. But generally, advertising religiously steers clear of saying what the precise contribution the product or service we want will make towards that end, lest we tot up the sums and discover that if everybody wanted "to make a stand for the planet" and bought a Lexus RX400H, we'd still be stuffed. As long as advertising's appeal follows the dictates of consumer psychology and is addressed to the individual then individual purchase decisions are much less likely to be based on what forms our communal good. A shopper's walk through a shopping mall is never accompanied by messages quantifying what your share is, only that you must have your share, which will be determined by the level of satisfaction it gives you. This is not to say that a greater awareness of our consumer society's impact on the environment is impossible, nor that the basic message will not get through; what it means is that whilst the dominant philosophy underlying the message is still entirely about individual satisfaction, it will appear counter-intuitive to act on messages which seek to make an imperative out of something which for most consumers remains inimical to consumption and is in any case perceived to be too remote to influence an immediate judgement about what is good or bad. Thus, the laudable Defra 'ActOnCO$_2$' campaign, appealing to us all to reduce our carbon footprint will have minimal impacts at the macro level, even if it may marginally alter a significant minority's behaviour. It has too few resources to compete with the larger narrative and worse, conveys the message that acting 'on CO$_2$' is merely a voluntary activity. Total advertising spend in the UK in 2007 was £19.4bn – admittedly not all of this was spent on advertising consumer goods and services - whereas over the period of three years from 2005 the government's 'Mass Communications' exercise on promoting climate change awareness (now called 'Act On CO_2') was given a budget of just £12 million. One might ask how much of an indulgence in counter intuitive thinking this is, no matter how well intentioned.[9]

The politics of our consumerist age inevitably lead politicians to make an unspoken (although it's never far below the surface) political Hippocratic Oath to the voter: we will make your life good (or failing that, better). This is now generally understood to mean materially better, a rather narrower definition perhaps than Jeremy Bentham spoke of when he suggested society should strive for the greatest happiness for the greatest number of people. Now we all want to report as Harold Macmillan did:

> Let us be frank about it: most of our people have never had it so good. Go around the country, go to the industrial towns, go to the farms, and you'll see a state of prosperity such as we have never had in my lifetime – nor indeed in the history of this country.

Macmillan's 'never had it so good' Gospel nevertheless came with a hint of The Revelation, as he continued:

> What is beginning to worry some of us is 'Is it too good to be true?' or perhaps I should say 'Is it too good to last?'[10]

Isn't it curious how what became Macmillan's most famous quote was not "Is it too good to last?" but 'You've never had it so good.' The desire to test the basis for material well-being may reveal a nervousness about its foundations, a persistent theme which seems to have come to the fore again as Gordon Brown's claims to ending 'boom and bust' (equivalent to 'you've never had it so good') have ended unceremoniously in what appears to be bust. Conveying the message that wellbeing may not last whilst seeking to affirm positive actions on climate change is thus a new challenge to the traditional political Hippocratic Oath, and to help devise a strategy of positive affirmation on climate change which could also fend off fatalism, Defra turned to the Futerra consultancy to examine how these diverging psychological paths could be reconciled. Solitaire Townsend of Futerra summed up how she thought the problem needed addressing:

> Changing behaviours in response to climate change should be easy. The issue is more worrying than terrorism, with direct implications for every household in the country. Even giving a moment's thought about the threat should have every one of us clamouring for our cavity walls to be filled, fighting in the aisles for the last energy saving light bulb and letting our cars rust in the driveway. The role of communications should surely be to simply make sure each member of the public takes that moment of thought. Here's the rub: the general public have had that moment of thought. The latest government research shows that 97 per cent of those surveyed recognised climate change and 71 per cent thought it was already affecting them directly or would do so in the next 20 years. But a laughingly small number have done a damn thing about it. Properly answering the question 'why' strays into the realm of philosophy. But the answer to the question 'what can we do about it?' thankfully results in some practical answers."[11]

Yes indeed: there are some very practical and for that matter cost-free (not even cost free: cost beneficial) answers, but still we generally do not take them. One might assume that MPs – our legislators – would have more of a handle on this since they might be more aware of the problem, but with some notable exceptions they are but representative of the population at large. Their general inability to switch lights off is not entirely their fault, since whole corridors in the Palace of Westminster do not appear to have light switches, but since every computer screen in the House of Commons library has a sticker on it saying 'Switch off after use' one might hope for some evidence here that the little, pain-free steps could be taken to reduce electricity consumption. Sadly not – one rarely comes to a machine where the screen has to be switched on again. After time, the weary act of switching lights off when they are clearly unnecessary becomes an act of social eccentricity, a civic duty in an age which doesn't appear to prize it – or prefers to delegate civic duty to others.

We have to move beyond the starting point that '97 per cent of the population recognise climate change' to 100 per cent of the population will do something about it. After years of 'recognising' climate change, as Solitaire Townsend says, "a laughingly small number have done a damn thing about it." Opinion polling on climate change and on the environment consistently show that knowing about climate change leads to its own inverted variation of psychologist Abraham Maslow's hierarchy of need, "What we now know as the Abraham Maslow hierarchy of need theory dates, in its initial conception, from circa 1943. This concept is applied to Human Beings and suggests that basic needs takes precedence but, once these are met, other needs come to the fore in people's lives. The most basic need is related to physiological survival - air to breathe, water to drink, food to eat and sex to procreate. Next in order of precedence comes a set of needs for such things as safety and security. Once an individual has taken care of his or her basic physiological needs and feels safe and secure some degree of need for love and belonging may well rise to the forefront of their concerns. Need for the respect of our fellow's, and for self-respect, are seen as being next in order of precedence." in which my need to do something comes last: after government, big business, NGOs, society at large, other individuals such as 4X4 drivers, those who live in large houses (or who have several houses), people who fly, and of course people who in Calor Gas' lovely phrase lead an 'alfresco lifestyle.'[12]

The problem of moving from climate change recognition to climate change action is compounded by the strength of that recognition. Whilst recent commentators have used polling evidence to query whether in times of economic gloom the public are more likely to lose their environmental concerns, there is evidence that one element of that change of opinion will be increasing doubt about the science of climate change, in other words it will help justify not doing anything about something if you deny its existence in the first place. Thus, a recent poll by IPSOS-Mori found that 60 per cent agreed with the proposition "many scientific experts still question if humans are contributing to climate change" and only 22 per cent disagreed.[13] This contrasts with other polls taken two or three years earlier which showed acceptance of the science of climate change hovering just above 50 per cent.[14] Whilst battening down the economic hatches may explain this change, it seems plausible too that the sceptical message, e.g. TV programmes like The Great Global Warming Swindle may also have had an impact, even if during the same period Al Gore's An Inconvenient Truth was winning much attention; but more likely is the empirical nature of climate change as experienced by people in their lives, which is to say that even after 20 or 30 years of climate change warnings from scientists, not much has happened yet which has affected people as they live – at least in the developed world. The proximate nature of the problem must be an influential factor, even if as IPSOS Mori found in July, 2008 77 per cent of survey respondents said that they were 'fairly' or 'very' concerned about climate change. The exact same percentage agreed with the statement "people say they're concerned but at the end of the day they're not prepared to make big sacrifices for the environment.'[15]

Talking about doing something has led to headlines like "Most Britons willing to pay green taxes to save the environment" whereas the reality belies these good intentions.[16] When asked "what is the number one thing you are doing to climate change?" IPSOS found that "I am not doing anything" was the number one answer, which combined with the "Don't knows" brought the total level of indifference to 59 per cent. The next most popular response was recycling at 23 per cent, followed by other activities most of which barely registered and could all be said to be less than a normal margin of error.[17] Analysing these results, Phil Downing of IPSOS-Mori drew the most positive interpretation he could in the circumstances: "As sobering as this may be, there remains plenty of cause for optimism. Environmental communications and marketing have come a long way – products and PR now trade on quality and novelty rather than guilt, and preaching is so 1990s. Moreover . . . sustainable homes are now associated with words like 'high tech' and 'comfortable,' shedding any preconceptions of worthiness. Neither do eco cars make the driver a social pariah like they used to, and so this repositioning of environmentalism as "smart living" and "eco chic" appears to offer considerable mileage if one forgives the pun."[18]

The problem with this analysis, which reflects the growing conventional wisdom of urging informed voluntaryism, is simply that it is not enough by a long chalk. If the Lexus RX400H is anything to go by, then our estimate of the success of achieving an 'eco chic' solution to the problem of climate change can be rated close to zero – no matter that eco-chic solutions, even if they are measured against their previous less climate friendly incarnations are improvements. This soft PR approach has to be accompanied by a harder appraisal of where we need to be. The value of the soft approach can only be of value if it helps sell the hard approach, which will not be voluntary but mandatory. But we do not seem to be ready for this step yet. Every effort is being made to search for new paradigms of voluntaryism in order to deflect taking stern action to stop the acknowledged looming catastrophe. George Osborne, the Conservative Shadow Chancellor has written warmly of a book called Nudge, by American author Richard Thaler, which says that 'we can nudge people to act more responsibly.' This is presented as some kind of revolutionary new thinking which could lead to policies "that will work in a post-bureaucratic age where Labour's clunking tax and regulation measures have all too often failed." Self-empowerment has to be good, and the greater availability of information in the market place will do no harm – but will a 'special mark on their energy bill' enthuse consumers sufficiently to reduce their consumption more than the bottom line? The long and complex route to what appears on the bottom line on an energy bill is likely to be more important, and state intervention has to have a much greater role to play in that. No weapon in the armoury should be discarded, but policies which are based on soft incrementalism will generally be too slow on their own to deliver a solution, and they can do nothing, by way of an aside, to assist our case in the hard nosed reality of international climate change politics: that demands greater assurances in a matter of months (this is written as we approach the half way mark on the 'Bali Roadmap'), not years.

Another major drawback of the 'nudge' philosophy is that it may further confuse the public, and if there is one thing we can learn from all the contradictory opinion poll results on climate change in recent years it is that the public is confused, or some may say fickle. However, one of the themes which does regularly emerge from opinion polls with some consistency is that the public expects the government to take strong action (already alluded to above in the context of an inverse hierarchy of need). To varying degrees people will say that they would accept higher taxes (cf the Guardian headline from 2006 or more recently a poll published in July 2008 which showed 63 per cent 'would support the introduction of green taxes')[19] But there's a but, which is when asked "do you think green taxes should be introduced irrespective of the present economic problems, 31 per cent said no to green taxes at all and 36 per cent wanted to delay their introduction. So if the government backs off taking tough decisions, and taxes usually fall within that category, are the public expected to believe that the matter is as serious as it's made out to be? Should they be expected to believe the rhetoric about a 'catastrophic' future if they can merely nudge it aside? By November 2008 it was reported that the Conservatives at least were growing cooler on the issue of green taxation.

Fear of public opinion has curtailed or at least stunted government policy on climate change since the fuel protests of 2000. For two or three torrid weeks, the government's opinion poll ratings fell below those of the Conservatives, for the only time in over a decade. There is no better brake on firm action than fear of a backlash, predicated on a fatalistic tautology which says: 'if we're not in power, then we can't do anything anyway.'

Hence, as we have seen much of the emphasis on compulsory climate change action has been 'upstream,' that is directed at businesses and entities which a) do not have votes and b) can pass their extra carbon abatement costs on to others. This means that for the consumer the carbon accountancy trail is masked or lost altogether. The irony of this is that consumers may end up paying for the same thing over and over again without realising it. Take the purchase of 'green' electricity for example: if you are a customer of one of the producers of 100 per cent renewable electricity in the UK, you may have to pay a premium for your power; but your bill will also include an amount which reflects the market in renewable energy created by the government's renewable obligation system, which mandates a specified level of generation from renewables (or a buy-out penalty if the generators don't reach their target); then you will have to pay the extra costs associated with the EU ETS, which means that power suppliers have to reduce their emissions or pay another penalty. Harnessed within this panoply of costs the consumer wanders, poorly informed of and certainly not recruited to the cause but paying for it anyway (uninformed except perhaps for the very small handful – there are around 200,000 customers who elect to have a green tariff of any description, never mind the 100% renewable tariffs). In the meantime, industry chunters on that it is 'running out of scope to curb their carbon dioxide output,' which may sound like a familiar strain, but what if there was a grain of truth to it? What then?[20]

The answer is unclear, and if all the measures we have in place still don't get our GHG emissions down to the level they should be at, further steps will be necessary – steps which will inevitably encroach upon some of our cherished consumer freedoms.

Ultimately this will mean some form of carbon rationing. It will mean that we will have to literally account for all of the embedded GHG emissions in what we consume, and the overall national carbon account will be capped each year, with the cap reducing as the circumstances dictate. The simplest calculation of that cap would be made using the Contraction and Convergence methodology, combining the science of climate change with an obvious distributional mechanism, based on global per capita shares by a set date. The problem with not adopting the personal carbon allowance (PCA) approach is that the responsibility for reducing GHG emissions is never handed to the end user, where the ultimate responsibility for consumption lies. We fear that the age of buck-passing would end with a jolt, as people were forced to wake up to the realities of carbon budgeting for the complete impact of their chosen lifestyle. The age of 'are you doing your little bit' (to paraphrase ActOnCO$_2$'s aborted climate change campaign predecessor) would be turned into the age of simply doing your complete bit.

That we individually should be conscious of and responsible for our own impact on the environment seems morally watertight, as well as being a lot simpler than having a multitude of different schemes, based on taxation, regulation and markets which inevitably result in double or even triple carbon accounting. But the path towards such a system is mired in difficulty – not least, of course, because of likely consumer (aka voter) resistance in the developed world. When opinion polls consistently show that people believe climate change is chiefly the government's problem to solve, it means there is a clear desire to delegate the whole problem to government too so that hopefully we will not notice the effort all that much. But it may also be because people recognise that if the government does it, there will be fewer options for escape for the free-loaders who so blight the prospects for successful voluntaryism. But then if government does get tough, what happens? We can throw them out and start all over again, and it remains the fault of government for not bringing in policies which are acceptable – acceptable that is to an electorate that has shown little interest in pursuing acceptable steps. Round and round we go.

An added layer of the moral justification for PCAs is the sheer inequity of who currently takes the 'blame' for GHG emissions. At the time of Kyoto and intensifying with the election of George Bush three years later, the United States was the world's favourite climate change bogeyman, but in more recent years – perhaps aided by deft manoeuvring by the US – China and to a lesser extent India are the blockages to progress, as their economies inexorably rise up the emitters' league table. Cynics can point to those countries and say that unless they do something, there's no point us doing anything – even though the vast bulk of Chinese goods are made for developed world markets and in the process have helped us enjoy a sustained mirage of economic well-being. But whose GHG emissions actually underpinned the lifestyles so endowed? Do these emissions belong to the producer or the consumer? Are we entitled to say that the Chinese, with low per capita emissions but now with the world's highest national

GHG output, should bear the cost of those emissions internally and not pass them on to us? This dilemma brings home one of the major problems encapsulated in the Kyoto Protocol, where the form of accounting is based on production, not consumption. Thus, whilst the UK can rightly point to the fact that our emissions (excluding aviation and shipping) are on target to hit and even exceed our commitments under Kyoto, research commissioned by Defra has shown that actually our embedded GHG emissions have risen quite dramatically. Early results from this research reported that "Consumer emissions (CE) are significantly higher than producer emissions (PE) or the UNFCCC national total [for the UK]. In 2004, CE were 132 Mt or 21% higher than PE and over 200 Mt or 37% higher than the national total reported to the UNFCCC, including overseas territories. CO_2 emissions embedded in imports (EEI) are higher than emissions embedded in exports (EEE) for all years and there is a clear trend towards increasing EEI, which went up from 4.3% of producer emissions in 1997 to 21% in 2004."[21] None of this should come as a surprise, after all wealthy people consume more. In 2005, the top ten per cent of the world's population was responsible for 59 per cent of its consumption; the bottom 50 per cent of the world's population was responsible for a miserable 7.2 per cent.[22]

Thus when we hear the oft-repeated claim that China is building two new coal power stations a week, we need to ask on whose carbon inventory their emissions should appear. And we might treat with even greater scepticism the kind of comment White House environment spokesperson James Connaughton made when he 'hailed the stabilisation of [US] greenhouse gas output as a victory for the US policy of avoiding mandatory targets.' All he was alluding to was keeping US GHG emissions off the US balance sheet, a technicality that does absolutely nothing to reduce global GHG emissions and everything to fool people into believing that progress has been made even in the absence of a mandatory regime.

The present arrangements make it easier to pass the buck, to both claim the credit for doing something and blame others for doing nothing. We worship in the cathedrals of consumerism, filled with icons made in China and pray that judgement day if it ever comes may be bought off in instalments. But to paraphrase a James Bond movie title, judgement day never comes: it's here already. Thus in looking for a solution to the problem of marrying our contribution to climate change with a methodology of personal responsibility, I had a serendipitous moment of epiphany whilst listening to the 2004 New Year's Day edition of the Today programme, on which Dr Kevin Anderson of the Tyndall Centre had been invited to speak about domestic tradable quotas (DTQs), Perhaps the programme's producers thought the DTQs plan could cure an almighty hangover.

DTQs, originally conceived by David Fleming of the Lean Economy Institute, basically allocates each citizen with a carbon emissions allowance each year, which they can use as they wish. If somebody does not use all of their allowance, they can sell their surplus; if somebody uses more, they can buy what they need. Each year, everybody's individual allowance would be reduced according to what the whole nation's carbon allowance needed to be in order to meet our overall GHG targets. In collaboration with Kevin Anderson and Richard Starkey, also at Tyndall, and David Fleming I was able to present DTQs in the form of a private members bill to the House of Commons in the summer of 2004. At that time, I privately felt I would be satisfied if within five years the government took the idea seriously. The immediate signs were not promising, but in the absence of other solutions, and because Tyndall Centre had led a major study of DTQs (to be followed by an even bigger study by the Royal Society of Arts (RSA) DTQs began to gain traction, and eventually Defra had reached the point of including DTQs in a list of ideas for tackling climate change that was presented to Cabinet in 2005 (my only reference for this was being shown a grainy photocopy of the Cabinet paper which had been leaked a few days later). Whilst there was no recommendation, the idea had at least made it to the top table. With the arrival of David Miliband as Secretary of State for Defra, the idea picked up speed, now with a more user friendly title 'personal carbon allowances (PCAs). He announced that the government (meaning Defra) would look very seriously at the question – but a danger signal was immediately clear – PCAs were, Miliband said, an interesting 'thinkpiece.' Outside of Defra's curtilage, more powerful forces would have none of it. Even during the same week that Miliband had announced the examination of this thinkpiece, I attended a meeting at which a Treasury special advisor was telling the audience the idea was going nowhere – and it didn't take much prescience to know he was right.

That tells us something about the over-bearing authority of the Treasury, of course, but it also says much about the chances of getting anything past those who wish to control not only revenue and expenditure but the foundations of the tax base. PCAs would do very little for the Treasury's coffers, they would be separate from the Treasury's revenues streams. They are not a flexible fiscal instrument that can be used to help balance the budget. In a similar way, Treasury opposes the principle of hypothecating taxation because that too reduces their flexibility. It is worth dwelling on this issue for a moment since it a major fault of taxation (apart from the fact that people don't like paying it) in the climate change context that it is difficult to quantify what exactly the impact of any 'climate change tax' would be. I once asked the Treasury what impact the doubling of APD would be on reducing GHG emissions from aviation. To my astonishment I got a precise answer, astonishing because common sense would tell us that such a calculation had to be pure invention: there are far too many variables to take account of, not least the fact of aviation's exponential growth thanks to the budget airlines. APD doesn't seem to have put anybody off.[23] At least with hypothecation, whilst one might never know exactly what the impact of the tax was on reducing GHG emissions, it would nevertheless still be possible to demonstrate that £10 of green tax income was spent on £10 worth of green goods. On the other hand (and just to confuse matters) if a green tax was successful in reducing an environmental bad, then logically revenue would fall away the more successful it was. Since the revenue from green taxes has indeed been dropping over recent years, the government has claimed this to be a sign of success, by definition there must be less bad environmental activity taking place. But this can only mean other taxes will have to be increased to fill the hole, and people might well ask whether the green tax was actually a green tax at all. All these arguments have been rehearsed ad nausea in the light of the 2007/08 economic downturn, and the result has an almost inevitable ring to it – we'll pay for this green stuff, but later please.

These are complications for taxation but not for personal carbon allowances. In contrast PCAs offer a concept of brilliant simplicity, a predictable and orderly reduction of GHG emissions year-on-year, with flexibility in an enclosed system, independent of taxation and providing complete transparency between goals and delivery. Unfortunately, having been described as an interesting thinkpiece and having won no admirers in the Treasury, the fate of PCAs appears to have been sealed. The result of a study was published by Defra in May, 2008 which concluded 'personal carbon trading has potential to engage individuals in taking action to combat climate change, but is essentially ahead of its time and expected costs for implementation are high.'[24] Hillary Benn's endorsement of the study's finding that the idea was 'ahead of its time' was echoed by Conservative environment shadow Peter Ainsworth MP who said "This is a very interesting idea and although it does have potential we should proceed with care."[25] When something is 'ahead of its time' and 'we should proceed with care' what is meant is that it is politically dead in the water even if, as Ainsworth has said "the threat of climate change is real and potentially disastrous."[26] Of course we should proceed with care when something is ahead of its time, but the level of caution suggested here reveals a disturbing lack of urgency. The House of Commons Environmental Audit Committee published a report on PCAs at the same time as the government's announcement was made and committee chair and former Conservative environment minister Tim Yeo MP showed a greater willingness to press ahead: "We found that personal carbon trading has real potential to engage the population in the fight against climate change and to achieve significant emissions reductions in a progressive way . . The idea is a radical one. As such it inevitably faces some significant challenges in its development. It is important to meet these challenges. What we are asking the Government to do is to seize the reins on this, leading the debate and coordinating research."[27]   That, surely would not be asking too much – to lead a debate and co-ordinate research? But a conspiracy of silence seems to have enveloped the front benches and not just the government's: after all this really is radical stuff, asking people to at least start with the same share of our national carbon budget rather than carry on with the model we have grown used to, which has seen the poverty gap widen to levels not seen since Queen Victoria was on the throne. What are the obstacles which have so diminished the chances of PCAs making political headway?

"We don't want to alienate people and we want everyone to be on board." *(Peter Ainsworth MP)*

"The scheme would penalise those living in the countryside who were dependent on their cars, as well as the elderly or housebound who need to heat their homes in the day. Large families would suffer, as would those working at nights when little public transport is available. It would need to take into account the size of families, and their ages. There is huge potential for fraud." *(Anonymous critics quoted in the* Daily Telegraph*)*

"The Government has shown itself incapable of managing any huge, complex IT system." *(Matthew Elliott of the Taxpayers Alliance)* [28]

To take the last objection first, if we were to accept the Taxpayers Alliance argument then we would have a watertight argument against any new government IT project. This argument to date has not stopped the government from pursuing, for example, the introduction of identity cards, so it cannot be an argument the government itself would accept, and whilst the opposition parties love to point an accusatory finger at government IT incompetence, that is no guarantee that they would handle IT projects any better. Certainly major IT schemes will continue to play a growing role in government affairs. Defra's study said "No insurmountable technical barriers were identified to the introduction of a personal carbon trading scheme, however the costs identified are very significant. Estimates of the likely set-up costs of the type of scheme explored ranged between £700 million and £2 billion, and the running costs £1 – 2 billion per annum."[29] These costs are those directly attributable to the scheme, and do not include the benefits which would inevitably be found in savings in other programmes designed to reduce the nation's GHG emissions. Indeed, one might regard this level of expenditure as relatively small, given how much the government was prepared to pay (£215 million) to pump prime less than three dozen companies to participate in the UK carbon emissions trading scheme, with the intention of establishing the City as a carbon trading centre. Whilst there have occasionally been very big problems with the introduction of large government IT projects, the Taxpayers Alliance assertion is simply not true. If it were, we would have to revert to using 18th century technology, when wooden tallies were used to count revenues. The abolition and subsequent disposal of these led to the great fire which destroyed Parliament in 1834.

Peter Ainsworth's objection that we don't want to alienate people and want everyone to be on board sets the bar of acceptability at a very high level. Whatever we do some people are going to be alienated. These people, even if they accept that they have as much responsibility to reduce their carbon footprint as everybody else has will still hope that there may be some genuine exemption which applies to them. Special pleading never ceases – no doubt the lifeboat decks of the Titanic heard some heartrending cases. But there will be groups of people who do need assistance to live within their carbon budget. For example, people who live in rural areas certainly do have to rely on their cars, even more so as we continue to close local post offices and the economic model we employ continues with the centralisation of the availability of goods and services. But this is a curious objection to PCAs, because it assumes that our economic model is best left unchanged. Surely we should be looking for a synergy between campaigns to save post offices and improve public transport with the campaign for PCAs, rather than positing PCAs on the present car-dependent model? With oil prices high, motorists are already finding alternative ways of getting about – car sharing, planning ahead, making less shopping trips – this is not rocket science.[30] But what happens when prices ease? Despite the high price of fuel in 2008, the long term trend of motoring costs has been downwards relative to disposable income, and recent changes to behaviour may be seen by many as a temporary phenomenon.

The introduction of PCAs therefore should not be seen as an isolated policy, but one which institutionalises behavioural change. Most of the other 'special case' objections have their remedies – we have an abundance of measures which are designed to tackle fuel poverty for example – the most important of which are designed to reduce energy consumption through improved insulation, more energy efficient appliances and so on. Sadly the money for such work has been capped at too low a level, perhaps reflecting the fact that energy efficiency is not seen to be politically sexy. And some of the money is wasted if it merely means that more energy hungry appliances are introduced – the 'rebound' effect which is like a variation of Parkinson's Law - work [energy use] expands to fill the time available. Hence, even if the behavioural changes which are brought about by price spikes themselves do become embedded, the savings that are made may then be expended on another carbon intensive activity. Thus, whilst visiting the home of a constituent who had benefited from the government's energy efficiency 'Warmfront' programme, she told me that it was now easier to afford her wall-hanging 48 inch plasma-screen TV.

The 'large families would suffer' point seems a spurious argument. It contradicts the common sense view that two can live more cheaply than one, although with the 1960s 'nuclear' family now more atomised it is only to be expected that mum, dad and the kids will no longer all sit in the same room watching the same telly. Every bedroom will be equipped with its own computer and possibly TV too. Not for nothing are the carbon emissions from computing rising as fast as those from aviation. But a house of five will benefit from having only one heating system, and heating is the main use of energy in the home. People living on their own may complain that they are at an energy consumption disadvantage, rather than the other way round.

Special needs in any system, be it based on regulatory, fiscal or allowance methods will need special measures to meet them, and perhaps a combination of all three approaches will work always provided the carbon accounting trail is kept simple. The question is how quickly can any measure work? If as the IPCC suggests the developed world needs to peak then reduce its GHG emissions no later than 2015, will nibbling away at the problem do the trick? The speed with which we should be reducing our carbon footprint does not yet seem to have sunk into most people's consciousness. As it is, all the 'upstream' measures so far adopted have been a kind of avoidance strategy – avoiding an inevitable clash with unfettered consumerism, where 'unfettered' means not internalising the external costs of environmental degradation. The decision not merely to delay the introduction of PCAs, but to shelve them pending an open-ended analysis is political cowardice. We should have learnt by now that voluntaryism will not deliver the result we need in the timescale required. In 1939 "Within three weeks of declaring war on Germany, Neville Chamberlain's National Government introduced petrol rationing and apart from some grumblings in the motoring press there was no opposition. There was also very little public outcry when food rationing started in January 1940 or clothes rationing 18 months later," York University historian Dr Mark Roodhouse told the Yorkshire Post.[31] As he noted in a paper one of the driving forces behind rationing was shipping space, and the threat of a German naval blockade would reduce the volume of imports.[32] Perhaps today we should learn to conceptualise our consumption in terms of what 'shipping space' remains to carry our demands – it is the carrying capacity of our mother ship, Planet Earth which is being gobbled faster than it can replenish itself.

Notes
1. Vodafone press advertisement, circa 2005
2. *Financial Times*, 6th September 2005
3. *Financial Times*, 10th November 2005
4. *European Voice*, 15th-23rd September 2005
5. *Guardian*, 25th July 2008
6. *Responsible and safe usage of LPG Alfresco Appliances*, Calor Gas advisory leaflet, 2004
7. *Guardian*, 25th June 2008
8. *Daily Telegraph*, 1st July 2008
9. www.adassoc.org.uk/html/news_releases.html; Defra news release 16th February 2005
10. Antony Jay, ed. The Oxford Dictionary of Political Quotations, OUP Oxford 1996
11. Inside Track, Issue 16 Spring, Green Alliance, London 2007
12. from http://www.age-of-the-sage.org/psychology/maslow_hierarchy_need.html:
13. www.ipsos-mori.com accessed 15th July 2008

14. e.g. Climate Change Fact Sheet, Environmental and Energy Study Institute, 20th April 2006

15. IPSOS op cit

16. *Guardian*, 22nd February 2006

17. *Understanding Society*, IPSOS Mori, November 2007

18. *ibid*

19. *Guardian*, 2nd July 2008

20. *Financial Times*, 15th November 2005

21. Development of an embedded carbon emissions indicator, A research report to the Department for Environment, Food and Rural Affairs by the Stockholm Environment Institute and the University of Sydney, Defra June 2008 Project website: http://randd.defra.gov.uk

22. http://web.worldbank.org

23. The answer was $2.75MtCO_2$ a year by 2010, see Hansard for 18th December 2006

24. Defra press release at http://www.defra.gov.uk/news/2008/080508c.htm

25. *Daily Telegraph*, 27th May 2008

26. quoted on e-politix 27th January 2008, at www.ecoearth.info/shared/reader/welcome.aspx?

27. Daily Mail, 27th May 2008

28. All quoted in *Daily Telegraph*, 27th May 2008

29. *Synthesis report on the findings from Defra's pre-feasibility study into personal carbon trading*, Defra, April 2008

30. e.g. 'Car journeys fall by a fifth, AA says' in *Daily Telegraph*, 15th July 2008

31. *Yorkshire Post*, 21st May 2007

32. *Rationing returns: a solution to global warming?* at www.historyandpolicy.org/papers/policy-paper-54.html

7

consensus?

*In Washington, issues come and go with the political winds. And they
are generally covered through that prism: Who's up and who's down?
Which party benefits? Which party loses? But in these superficial
exchanges, we often lose sight of the real and lasting meaning of the
decisions we make and those we defer. The issue of climate change is one
that we ignore at our own peril.*

Senator Barack Obama[1]

What will it take to embed in our society the policies and actions
which will ensure we make our fair contribution to tackling
climate change? Can such policies and actions occur within a
political system which relies heavily on building popularity on
adversarial stand-offs and the continual denunciation of ideas
(as well as individuals) that emanate from outside the tribe? It
is not unknown for political parties to use each others' ideas, but
when this happens it is de rigueur to describe one's opponents
as thieves, to make the point that so bereft are they of their own
ideas that they must steal them from their opponents. It is a
matter of pride that you got there first, so that you can claim the
credit. This straightforward contest between two political fronts

has been somewhat eroded by the arrival (with Bill Clinton) in the 1990s of the strategy of triangulation, where one deliberately and openly adopts positions which appeal to different sectors of the electorate regardless of any party platform, leaving the opposition marginalised even on some of their own turf. Whilst triangulation may be a key tactic of an equivocating centrist approach, it seems an inadequate response to climate change, which demands a radical rethink of many of the assumptions underpinning societies in the developed world, assumptions which have rarely been addressed thoroughly by either traditions of the left or the right. Our access to resources as if they were infinite has been one of the chief assumptions that has hardly intruded in the debate between left and right – that debate has always been more defined by the distribution of resources in the shape of wealth then by the availability of what 'wealth' comprises.

It is almost impossible to envisage this approach changing, so deeply ingrained in the body politic is it. There are precedents for parties working together to address a serious challenge, the most notable example in British politics being the coalition government which Churchill formed in 1940. This came about when the Nazi threat had become so overwhelming that there seemed little alternative. The threat of invasion was not far off, a military debacle had just occurred in Norway and France was about to be overrun. But coalition had to wait until Chamberlain had ceased to be Prime Minister, quite some time after war had started. As contemporary records illustrate, there were still plenty of politicians around who questioned the need for coalition, who probably felt that Conservatives working with socialists (and vice versa) was a recipe for the demise of their own principles and thus their respective parties in the long run. Needless to say, some careerists too will be nonplussed by the sight of one's party offering or taking positions of power which might have come your way, but were now filled with opponents. All a hard act to swallow.

A more recent crisis – Ted Heath's struggle with energy policy in 1973/74 – which led to his instigating a three day working week in December, 1973 was the backdrop to a fascinating glimpse of the febrile nature of political principle and ambition, if Tony Benn's diary is to be believed:

[Thursday, 3rd January 1974]

I asked whether Michael Foot was right to compare our attitude to the situation in 1940 and 1945 because in 1940 Britain had a coalition Government, to which Jim [Callaghan] said. 'Well, I'm in favour of a national government.'

I repeated, 'A national Government?'

'Yes,' he confirmed, 'if it adopted our policy.'

'What - a coalition Government?'

'Yes, but I knew they wouldn't,' he said.

'What you are saying is that you would be in favour of excluding from the public the choice between two policies.'

'I think a coalition Government, a national Government, would be a good thing if it would follow our policy,' was his reply.

John Silkin had said to me before Christmas, that he thought Jim might be won over to a coalition Government; and John's theory was that Whitelaw – who had a great admiration for Jim – might offer him the premiership. I'd thought it a far-fetched idea, but this was a minor confirmation of it.[2]

Here are a group of people who had youthful memories of Ramsay MacDonald's 'great betrayal' in 1931 now contemplating not only the presumed departure of Harold Wilson as leader of the Labour Party but throwing their hand in with the Conservatives in one of the most fractious periods of recent British history. Heath had already called a state of emergency, the three day week was biting and he was asking the fateful question 'who governs Britain?' From the above conversation it is clear that the Conservatives, who after all were in government with a working majority that could maintain them in office until 1975, could not have accepted the terms Callaghan outlined. But at least in some people's minds the possibility of national government could be entertained, always provided 'we' led it and it was based on 'our principles.' Labour went on to win the February, 1974 election in its own right, albeit with a single figure majority, so perhaps afterwards Callaghan's ruminations will have been downplayed and quickly forgotten. In any case the crisis was essentially short-term in nature, a human engineered energy 'crunch' rather than an all-enveloping, long-term environmental catastrophe. Much later, Heath wrote "I find that nowadays people are astonished to learn that production fell by less than 2 per cent during the three-day week. This showed how much better industrial performance could, and should, have been at normal times."[3] On one reading then every cloud has a silver lining, but this was the last time that a coalition government was actively discussed in the UK in response to events, rather than for anticipated political convenience. It is true that Callaghan did go on with David Steel to form the Lib-Lab pact (not a coalition) to maintain a government with a slender majority in power; a similar pact was discussed between Tony Blair and Paddy Ashdown prior to 1997, but Labour's landslide finished that idea off. A loose consensus existed between the parties over the Northern Ireland peace process prior to and following the Good Friday Agreement, but since the main parties did not at that time contest Northern Ireland elections, perhaps this did not demand too much effort.

What might be the steps required today to achieve an alliance between political parties of sufficient strength and resilience that it could deliver the radical policies that inevitably will be needed to drastically reduce our dependence on fossil fuels? An end to the political culture of cognitive dissonance might be a good place to start, beginning with the relaxation of all the rules of tribal political engagement. This need not be so hard, and indeed there are many examples, some already alluded to in the previous paragraph, where parties can conceive of working together. But there are plenty of other examples: many local authorities are run by cross party coalitions, the Labour administrations in the first Scottish parliaments were coalitions as indeed is the current Welsh administration; much of the work of the cross-party select committees in the House of Commons are based on thematic rather than partisan analysis, and most of these committees pride themselves on their non-partisan approach. Sometimes – and this will come as no surprise - it seems as if the adversarial yah-booing exemplified at Prime Minister's question time is merely a show, devised purely for the benefit of partisan morale.

This yah-booing when applied to actual policies, rather than the Prime Minister's or opposition leader's hair style or sweatiness is an essential foundation for non-reflective, iterative policy development. Hence, when a policy is adopted by one side, it becomes that much more difficult to amend the more it is attacked by the other; or if it is adjusted, that adjustment must be presented as if it were the consequence of some internal review which pre-dated (of course) the opposition's fulminations. A recent example of this latter behaviour was the government's changes to inheritance tax, which appeared after the Shadow Chancellor George Osborne made a successful speech to the Conservative Party conference in 2007. A long-standing policy, the Climate Change Levy has so far resisted such a change, even though some of its inadequacies are showing through.[4] Whenever climate policy is discussed, we will be told by ministers that the opposition is against tough action 'because they oppose the Climate Change Levy.' But what if the opposition's (or somebody else's) policy was actually better? Once you've settled on your policy, it's too late, all the others must be full of holes (but this can change if a new policy can be so repackaged, a la inheritance tax, to appear as being of one's own invention). And perhaps triangulation does not work so well with environmental policies – if environmental concerns are not high on the electorate's agenda, and as we have seen generally they are not, then the environmental constituency has less traction, as compared to say law and order, immigration or health. The success or otherwise of an environmental policy like the Climate Change Levy may also be harder to pinpoint for the benefit of public consumption. To say for example that a policy may have saved 10 million tonnes of CO_2 will appear as meaningful to most people as if it had saved 100 million tonnes of CO_2. Any policy in this regard could be boasted of provided it had saved some CO_2 – the question is whether another policy may have saved more. But for the average onlooker, the debate will have as much resonance as watching paint dry.

To break out of this padded political cell requires courage. It may, indeed probably most definitely will mean abandoning tribal loyalties, and risking the approbation of one's political kin, developed over many years. And if one lays down a challenge to all the political tribes one may find oneself so marginalised as to be without influence over any of them, unlike the floor-crosser who at least hopes for a welcome in his new tribe sufficient to obscure the contempt of his old one (all recent political ship-jumpers have been male). In considering the options for cross-party work outside of the formally approved structures, most approaches will be heavily constrained by the peer-group pressure which ensures that so-and-so may be considered a bit 'iffy.' Perversely, at the very highest reaches such behaviour may be classed as visionary, i.e. putting the nation before party, being selfless, motivated by a higher purpose and all that. Perhaps David Cameron's appeal to this higher purpose helped him win the Conservative leadership race when he said "That [wanting a programme on climate change designed for the next 50 years] requires a radically different approach – a change in how British politics has handled this issue up to now. We need to take the politics out of it: we need to constrain future governments in the face of the natural tendency to put short-term electoral considerations above the long term interests of the country and the planet." Which sounded good, but the Times news report's following paragraph had rival leadership contender David Davis MP saying that he alone offered the party real policy, not 'spin,' which in this context could equally have been a dig at Tony Blair's leadership on climate change, seen by many to be visionary but lacking in substance.[5]

Hoping to appeal to the soon-to-retire Prime Minister's visionary side, I was inspired in 2006 to present to Tony Blair the All Party Parliamentary Climate Change Group's (APPCCG) report on the possibilities for a cross party consensus which was published in July that year. From a tribal perspective, it was my view that whoever took a lead in forming such a consensus would reap a benefit that could, ironically, only help their own party. To the extent that it is true that the public want to see positive role models in politics rather than negative attacks, then true consensus should beat cynical triangulation any day. For a Prime Minister contemplating his legacy, and one who had the previous year made so much of climate change at the G8 summit at Gleneagles, this could have been an opportunity to demonstrate how a world statesman makes good his pledges at home. Why should such an appeal not work? Much is made of the deleterious impacts to political parties which suffer internal divisions – does the same rule not apply to what happens between parties? A unifying process, building cross party consensus on a very difficult and complex issue could impress the electorate. My meeting with Tony Blair (which followed the Andy Warhol 15 minutes of fame rule) allowed me to introduce the report to him, and it seemed he may have been interested, interested enough anyway to sound sympathetic although not really interested enough to suggest a further meeting or some follow-up action. It was hard to divine whether I should or could say to others 'this has Tony's approval.' I left him a copy of the APPCCG report with little expectation that anything more would happen. The meeting took place at a time when some Labour backbenchers were agitating to get rid of him. For them I doubt if some noble intent to create a cross-party consensus would have seemed very attractive – their concerns were to refocus on attacking the Tories, not to get into bed with them. Tribalism nearly always trumps alliances (barring my enemy's enemy is my friend type alliances, of course), even when it comes to those alliances which could embed our own values in the rather less than minor matter of saving the species.

The APPCCG report, which resulted from a five month inquiry modelled on select committee lines, and written independently by Dr Helen Clayton, Prof. Nick Pidgeon and Prof. Mark Whitby, concluded that a cross party consensus was a necessary condition if radical climate change policies were to be introduced. They found that there was at that time at least a rhetorical commitment to a consensus approach. A remark by Peter Ainsworth MP, the Shadow Environment Minister, prompted David Miliband, then Secretary of State for Defra to say "If we can forge a consensus and if the new model Conservative Party wants to see the light, I will welcome them to the consensus table."[6] Of course, put like that the invitation could be accepted as disingenuously as it was assumed to be made, and this illustrates yet again how what we may call the Callaghan principles of consensus are still applied: consensus will work under my leadership according to my principles. And yet, as Clayton et al noted, in the government's Climate Change Programme of 2006, it stated "Internationally we will: work to build a consensus on the scale of action needed to stabilise the climate and avoid dangerous climate change, and build on the progress made at the G8 Summit in Gleneagles and the Montreal climate change conference to strengthen the international regime."[7] Could a consensus at the international level then be a more opportune affair, available only to those who already hold the reins of power at any given time? If so, then it could be short-lived.

All the opposition parties represented in the House of Commons in January, 2006 had signed up to their own consensus statement – the Joint Statement on a Cross-Party Approach to Climate Change, and it was Ainsworth's invitation to sign up to this which had so filled Miliband with faux enthusiasm. The opposition statement accepted the science of climate change, and declared that "We believe that normal politics is simply not delivering the actions necessary to tackle this threat." It proposed "the establishment of a new, independent, authoritative body with a specific remit to: set binding annual targets, to secure reductions in UK greenhouse gas emissions and monitor progress towards them; advance measures to achieve year on year reductions in climate change gas emissions; publish a report annually on its findings which will trigger an annual debate on the floor of both Houses of Parliament on the report; and develop policy measures in the light of changes in scientific evidence." The joint statement went on to commit the parties to "work together to develop specific joint policy proposals, seeking agreement wherever possible" and to establish a Climate Change Forum, comprising members of each Party, which will meet regularly to take this initiative forward."[8]

But it was not to be. One of the initiators of the joint statement, Norman Baker MP was moved sideways from his Liberal Democrat environment position, to be replaced by Chris Huhne MP – a change which occurred at the same time that the APPCCG inquiry into cross-party consensus was getting underway. In seeking to formulate their joint response to the inquiry the opposition parties fell out with each other, possibly due to Huhne's reluctance to agree with the Conservatives on tax measures, although the demise of the opposition agreement was never properly explained – nor was it clear that all the parties were party to the ending of it.

The lesson to be drawn from the brief life of this experiment in cross-party consensus was that it has to be rigorous and robust enough to withstand the hazards of the 'devil in the detail.' Just because we all agree climate change is happening and it's very, very nasty does not automatically translate into 'and here is our joint statement on carbon taxation policy.' In the event, some of the things called for in the opposition joint statement have with some approximation been dropped into the Climate Change Act: an independent and authoritative Climate Change Committee will indeed make annual reports to Parliament on items not entirely dissimilar to those the joint statement recommended. However, differences remain and they may still be pointed to as examples of government perfidy, following the usual, necessarily political path which fits Sigmund Freud's description of the ego of small differences. But that there could be room for positive development, rather than simple inter-party name calling may be indicated by the fact that the joint statement called for cuts in greenhouse gas emissions of 60% - a figure replicated in the Climate Change Act and which is now universally agreed to be much too little.

The recommendations of the APPCCG inquiry contained various structural approaches to confidence building – such as giving the government's Office of Climate Change some remit in consulting other parties, as well as setting up a Monetary Policy Committee-like body to agree targets and so on. No doubt such a body would be able to take evidence from all sources. But I would go further. If we are to tackle the dilemma that Tony Benn identified in his reference to Callaghan's alleged dream "of excluding from the public the choice between two parties" and we want effective policies which won't be watered down (even with cross party support, the government party of the day is still the only one which will be punished at the next election for unpopular policies and will therefore be under more pressure) there needs to be a process which carries electoral legitimacy. This is where we get into interesting territory, since this could only realistically be achieved through the presentation at an election of a joint manifesto, or perhaps a process which involves a referendum. Both options will attract the charge that some form of 'eco-fascism' is being imposed – we will hear of the return of corporatism, the end of democracy and so on. Such charges will have to be weighed against the alternatives – perhaps one of the Foresight scenarios, for example? Also, there will be a chorus of censure based on the presumption that if the UK went ahead with this project domestically before the rest of the world joined us in taking the presumed tough actions such political action presupposes, then we would be trying to take the whole burden on to ourselves when, as it is often (wrongly) alleged, we only contribute two per cent of the problem. This latter argument is often used in favour of doing nothing (not even a two per cent effort) since whatever we do will be swamped by the results of a lack of climate change mitigation elsewhere.

The first option – a joint manifesto – is perhaps not a separate option at all, since the general election would effectively be a referendum on that. But in the context of a general election, the voters would still have a choice – in whom they trust most to be in government to ensure that the consensus is maintained. That choice would not be offered in a referendum, since it would be conducted by the government of the day. The question of whether a failure to win the referendum should lead to some sort of vote of confidence may then arise, although it is hard to see - except on the superficial issue of a failure of process - how the opposition parties could capitalise on this situation. If the unity amongst parties survived a referendum defeat, then we may see the proposition re-presented at a later date in an amended form (what we might call the Irish option) or perhaps the parties if they remain fully committed may just get on with implementing their policies anyway. In the words of one leading Conservative environmentalist, "what is necessary is what is practical. If being practical is doing less than what is necessary, then it is likely to end in failure."[9] In a sense, a 'climate change' referendum would be a shallow exercise in democracy – there is no choice but to take the difficult steps to rapidly decarbonise the economy, and a 'no' vote would be ignored by nature.

What are the chances even in the absence of the approaches outlined above, that the parties may at least converge more accidentally onto the same territory? Convergence is a perquisite of consensus. In this regard there are perhaps some signs of hope, although to shine a light on this possibility is to dare the actors to leave the stage lest they appear too accommodating of their opponents. In the run-up to any general election, tradition demands that all ministers and their shadows are charged with the responsibility of defining difference, not exposing similarity – and this often means keeping your cards close to your chest until the other side has revealed theirs.

A glance at the Conservative Party's webpages on the 28th July 2008 – a day after David Cameron had challenged Gordon Brown to call a general election in the wake of Labour's Glasgow East by-election drubbing - revealed a startling hole in the Conservatives' readiness to promote a coherent environmental message. Following through links to 'Our Policies' one was taken to "Our Security Agenda" where, the viewer is told "We have a clear vision of the Britain we want to see: a country where people have more opportunity and power over their lives; where families are stronger and society is m ore responsible; a Britain which is safer and greener. In the months ahead, we will set out in detail how we plan to make a reality of this vision when we get into government. We will be publishing a series of Policy Green Papers around three core visions for Britain."[10] But as of the 28th July, only prison reform merited a detailed statement under the 'safer and greener' page; the far more difficult question of the environment did not merit a single word, and indeed nor had it for at least the previous three months (I only monitored the site for that length of time). Of course, elsewhere on the Conservative website there are many mentions of green policies, but a single coherent vision evidently was not yet available despite the fact that immediately upon becoming Conservative leader, David Cameron had majored on his environmental concerns. True, by the 21st November 2008, more information was posted to the website, and although it still seemed to be on a par with prison policy we could nevertheless learn more about Conservative energy policy, coincidentally just as a major plank of the government's energy policy – in the form of a Bill - was passing through its final stages.

One of the reasons for this incoherence has to be about keeping options open – to better oppose the government as the need arises in a point scoring (as measured in opinion polls) exercise which both sides engage in. Take two examples. In June, 2008, under the headline "I won't back Gordon's great Heathrow con" David Cameron explained to *Evening Standard* readers:

> The Prime Minister has noticed that since I became leader of the Conservative Party, I have pushed the environment higher up the political agenda. But rather than engage with the green agenda, either driving it forward in government or indeed openly rejecting it, he has decided to play politics with it. So he tries to define the issue of a third runway as a "tough choice"

between the economy and the environment. If you back a third runway you're on the side of jobs, business and prosperity. If you don't, you're somehow not serious, putting lightweight environmental concerns ahead of the economy." [11]

These are indeed challenging battle lines, especially at a time of economic downturn. But Cameron's calculation is finely honed to particular audiences. Contrast his opposition to a third runway (*inter alia*, the growth of aviation) with this:

Some Labour MPs now seem to realise that they are fast approaching high noon for their lop-sided green strategy. Over the last decade, Labour has pursued a dogged and unpleasant campaign attacking the motor vehicle in all its guises. The car has been castigated as it were the main generator of carbon dioxide, attacked for being unsafe, and singled out to be one part of the economy which must not grow." [12]

That was John Redwood MP, Chairman of the Conservative Party's policy group on economic competitiveness, telling *Yorkshire Post* readers in May, 2008 about the government's "crippling taxes on motor vehicles and fuel." Whilst Redwood warns his readers of the government's "environmental horror movie" his real intent is merely to ensure that foreign hauliers do not have a competitive advantage over ours – a reasonable case, but one which tells us little (or maybe rather too much) about the Conservatives' environmental strategy. At Heathrow, the prescription is to make it "better not bigger. That means looking seriously at competition issues surrounding BAA and how our airports are managed." [13] No harm in that one might think, except that it is not a proposal to curb the growth in aviation's greenhouse gas emissions – that presumably will happen in some other way. It is however a proposal to make the operation more efficient, so allowing more passengers to make more of existing facilities – a plan for GHG growth in all but name. To counter that Cameron's article revealed how he had developed a 'Blue/Green Charter' which comprised five elements: "We should boost technological change by harnessing the power of the markets and innovation;" "Green taxes should be replacement taxes, not new ones;" "to keep the lights on by securing our energy supplies" (this made reference to "a new system of decentralised energy" and implicitly a feed-in tariff); "We must prioritise energy efficiency;" and lastly "getting transport right" which means "finding ways to unlock our transport infrastructure and get Britain moving."

All of which is laudable, but in many ways unexceptional. Clearly there are things we should be doing such as introducing the feed-in tariff adopted by most EU countries to support renewable energy, which in study after study has been found to be more effective than the UK's quota system. But with the Conservatives and Labour both meeting eye to eye on building a new fleet of nuclear power stations, there must remain a very large doubt as to whether either party has a coherent energy strategy. It is hard to see how a 'system of decentralised energy' sits comfortably with the biggest, least flexible energy beasts of our current, highly centralised system. Nuclear power is anathema to decentralisation.

Seeking a comprehensive, meaningful consensus from a starting point of agreement on policies – the 'devil's in the detail' sort of stuff – is doomed to failure, because details make such a poor starting point for cross-party confidence building. Even within the Conservative Party, the pressures between the pro-competition evangelists and those who favour stricter controls to achieve environmental goals are difficult to reconcile. This much was powerfully acknowledged by Nick Hurd MP, a member of the Conservative Party's Quality of Life Commission, who with Clare Kerr published a report in 2006 entitled "Don't give up on 2°"

> "We cannot hide behind lazy arguments on cost and competitiveness when we are so manifestly complacent about how we deploy capital and taxpayers money. Both the Government (Gershon Report) and the Conservatives (James Report) went into the last election with messages of chronic wasteful spending in the public sector, ranging from £21bn to £35bn per annum. We appear to be drifting into decisions about nuclear power, about Trident, about the super sewer, just as we drifted into decisions about the Iraq war without any meaningful public debate. A 2004 report from the New Economics Foundation claims that global fossil fuel subsidies amount to approximately $235 billion a year. Diverting a small fraction of that money to renewable energy would make an enormous difference. Every year the government gives some £6 to £8 in fossil fuel subsidies for every £1 to support clean and renewable energy, and a typical British taxpayer pays at least £1,000 a year to fund perverse subsidies. Surely it is time to bury the past and invest in conserving the future?"[14]

'Lazy arguments . . on competitiveness' combined with an interventionist approach of switching subsidies to renewable energy? What appears as an attack on the government is perhaps a significant if coded warning to the Redwood wing of the Conservative Party too to wake up to the looming environmental crisis. If so, then it would be welcome. Here is a view from the left of the Conservative Party which has not yet been reconciled to its dominant philosophy.

As things stand there is perhaps more unanimity between the parties in their common view that the state should be an enabler rather than an interventionist, the state's job being to tweak the markets with signals and hope that they respond positively. Given the urgency of tackling climate change, this approach has some obvious drawbacks, not least of which is the fact that such a policy may allow for enormous 'leakage' if too many market participants can avoid compliance with government policy, and if there are too few market or state penalties for evasion or indeed fraud.

The interventionist debate entered a new phase in autumn 2008 with concerns over high domestic fuel prices being intertwined with the future of Gordon Brown's premiership. The debate about whether Labour should impose a windfall tax on the energy companies illustrated how social and environmental goals were being jumbled together, with social objectives appearing to demand the more urgent attention. Within the Labour 'broad church,' superficially so ideologically united since Blair became leader, the stresses between pro-market and pro-interventionist factions became apparent.

Labour's fuel poverty targets were amongst the first of its social targets to be introduced in 1997. One of the government's first acts was to cut the rate of VAT on fuel from 17.5 per cent to five per cent, the lowest level allowed under EU law. But ten years on, in the face of international energy price rises, that record on fuel poverty was kicked into a cocked hat, a hat with which appeared Gordon Brown went begging to the power companies for assistance in late summer 2008, with the rather remote threat of a windfall tax up his sleeve should it come to that.

Labour's light touch policy structure for many years looked impressive, so far as keeping energy prices down was concerned. Liberalisation had brought a long but temporary reduction in prices, allowing Ofgem to take a sedentary approach to its primary duty to ensure value for money through competition. Labour's Warmfront programme to make homes more energy efficient was making slow but steady progress. Less well-off people were getting assistance to reduce their energy bills. It hasn't taken very much to undo this good work.

A windfall tax could be an option to address this problem and appeared to be the first option sought by the left in the party. As a last resort it undoubtedly has to be held in the government's pack of cards in their negotiations with an industry which seems scandalised by the very thought that it has profiteered from recent price rises. But last resorts rarely make good deals, and the use of a windfall tax could merely compound the existing problem with the market, rather than solve it – and it is our excessively liberalised market that is the root of the problem. Is it not ironic that whilst we have the most liberalised energy market in Europe and the most recalcitrant largely foreign-owned energy industry to boot, the only response of the left has been to demand a windfall tax on their profits when what is needed is a root and branch review of the operation and ownership of the industry? If the left wanted to look really decisive, it could have demanded Gordon Brown followed Nicholas Sarkozy's example and tell the regulator to cap price increases to 5 per cent. EDF, an 85 per cent French state owned company was unlikely to turn round to Sarkozy and tell him their future investment in France was under threat, as the representatives of their British operators told the government here. The absence of calls for more state control of our energy supply is a curiously vacant space in British politics, perhaps as a consequence of the headline grabbing bank bail-outs, or part nationalisations in the 'credit crunch.'

A windfall tax to address fuel poverty would implicitly accept the current structure of the UK industry, and sends a signal that all is needed are occasional corrections. Such a tax could bring short term relief to those on low incomes, but what they need is long-term protection coupled with environmental sustainability. Where is the new thinking here? Perhaps we could begin by asking whether our ten year old fuel poverty target, which defines anyone spending more then ten per cent of their income as being fuel poor is still relevant. The target is only accidentally related to any environmental objective, even though it is often quoted as an environmental policy too.

We should have a new target which assesses the energy needs of families along with an assessment of the optimum energy performance of their home. Since energy efficiency measures often do not reduce energy consumption, but merely encourage the use of more energy consuming devices, we cannot simply assume that the level of energy usage reflects any form of poverty if it rises above a certain arbitrary point. The householder who has received several thousands of pounds worth of insulation, central heating and double glazing work should not then expect to be state assisted to watch a 60 inch plasma TV – or have I missed something? The definition of fuel poverty has to reflect what energy we need for our basic needs, such as heating and cooking, and not include every gadget that comes along which fleshes out predictions that we will never get our growth in energy consumption under control.

To this end the statutory duties energy providers are placed under need a radical overhaul. The long discussed but little developed concept of turning energy suppliers into energy service companies should be moved forward, obligating them to do a lot more than they now are to reduce their customers' demand – and pay for the measures necessary. But as we have seen with the non-introduction of smart metering, the electricity suppliers have successfully argued for delays to additional legal duties. The fact that until summer, 2008 the government had separate departments dealing with energy efficiency and energy supply did not help, especially when the latter half had so little understanding of the urgency of climate change.

As it stands, the windfall tax proposal is a great distraction. If it is posited as the saviour of Labour's fortunes it is an even worse distraction, taking attention away from the real causes of the party's current difficulties. There are structural issues that have to be dealt with – and the government still has time to make those changes, which would revise our new Labour's subservient attitude to markets. As it is, a reliance on 'signals' is likely to remain at the core policy, Labour of indeed Conservative.

If market 'signals' are to be strong enough (assuming markets will be the predominant route to carbon abatement) then there has to be more consensus between the political parties to ensure determination of purpose, continuity and policing. Here we must look to the Climate Change Act (CCA) for guidance. The principle of introducing the CCA has been welcomed on all sides of the House. And its core aims of setting targets and budgets, promoting carbon markets and the establishment of an 'authoritative' oversight body have been largely uncontroversial, at least amongst most

parliamentarians.[15]   There was perhaps significant evidence
of non-partisanship when the Bill arrived for clause by clause
scrutiny by MPs in committee. Two debates took around a
third of the committee's time, and considered whether the
Bill should have a principle aim, a new Clause One which had
been inserted by the opposition in the Lords and which sought
to express the Bill's overarching purpose as requiring the UK
to contribute proportionately to the global goal of keeping any
temperature increase to within 2°C; the second debate looked
at whether the 2050 carbon dioxide emissions reduction target
stated in the Bill should be increased from at least 60% to 80%.
The latter proposal had been widely sought by NGOs, experts
and political parties. Gordon Brown had even referred to an
80% target in his first party conference speech as leader in 2007,
re-iterated a year later and 80% was also stated Conservative
Party policy. Indeed, Brown had also said that the 2° limit was
'our overriding aim' in a speech in November, 2007. Against
this background, the debate was always going to have a surreal
air about it – on what terms could the parties find differences?

Speaking to the 2° proposal the former environment
secretary, John Gummer MP said:

> The nature of this Bill – this is why the Government should be
> congratulated – is to say to the world that we, at least, are a
> country that takes the matter seriously and that we will act in
> a way that is incumbent not only on the Government but on
> the Opposition. It is interesting that the commentators have
> not noticed that the Bill has a real effect on the Opposition
> as well as on the Government, because it will not be possible
> for an opposition of any kind merely to oppose things that the
> Government want to do in order to fulfil the purposes of the

Bill without providing a practical and real alternative. That makes the Bill very valuable; for the next two years' time, it will be very important when the situation is the other way round. It is crucial that we are all caught by the Bill. If that is the case, I want to be caught by the truth, and Clause 1 is an important part of the truth, which is that we have to commit ourselves to act, whatever anybody else does. Unless we do, and thereby inspire others as well, we will not achieve the necessary change sufficiently quickly. (emphasis added)[16]

What are normally unreported public bill standing committees can be echo chambers for the verbose, not least for some of the House's more loquacious members but Gummer's comments deserve attention since he recognised that the purpose of any climate change bill can only reflect our contribution to a global ambition (climate change being nothing less than global). But he also indicated that the problem was global in another sense, i.e. it is not an issue which can be tucked into separate and discrete political boxes, as perhaps one might dissect the issue of selection in education or how to pay for healthcare. Thus, his contention that the opposition (of whatever stripe) is locked into a – shall we say, progressive – effort means the abandonment of the long-held tradition that it is the primary task of Her Majesty's Official Opposition to oppose – a proposition which often enables the opposition leader to admonish the Prime Minister with a jobsworth's non-committal 'it's my turn to ask the questions' riposte anytime an inquiry is made of his or her own position. What we may now dub 'Gummer's Doctrine' – that the opposition is duty bound to proffer its genuine alternative when attacking the government's policy – would be a welcome step towards removing the automatic assumption that all we have to do in political discourse to prove our virility is to defeat the other side.

The Committee's deliberations on whether the UK's goal should be to take our fair share of responsibility for keeping the global temperature increase to within 2° led to a consensus that that indeed should be the case and differences persisted only on the question of where in the bill that objective should be placed – a legalistic, rather than a substantive issue even if at the end of the debate a vote was taken on the original wording – which the government won. Similarly with the move to an 80% reduction target – an amendment which was moved by a Labour member, David Chaytor MP - there was no disagreement on the desirability of such a move, the question revolved around the matter of process, not least what would be the 'independent' climate change committee's role in all of this? Who should decide what the correct figure should be – our independent experts, or politicians? And should politicians be bound to accept the figure arrived at by experts? Given that most speakers in the debate alluded to scientific reports, e.g. from the IPCC that 80% was correct, or from people like Sir Nick Stern who were saying the same thing, the politicians thought they were justified in putting 80% in the bill. If the outside world ever got to hear about the debate on the 24th June, 2008 they may like Steve Webb MP, the Liberal Democrat spokesperson on the committee have wondered where they were in Wonderland, since it appeared as if the government had the support of the opposition in preventing the Labour member's amendment reaching the statute book, even though everybody from the Prime Minister down agreed 80% was the better figure. The Climate Change Committee's task in considering the appropriateness of 80% was even accelerated by Gordon Brown to be complete before Royal Assent could be given to the Bill.

The Standing Committee's nuts and bolts examination of the Climate Change Bill revealed a substantial level of agreement between the parties, although one is tempted to ask: who will deliver the results? The impact of this legislation on other policies has yet to be felt, and other government departments could be likened to sleeping lambs unaware of the force which hopefully is about to hit them. This is where the calm pastures of cross party consensus will be most thoroughly tested. Perhaps we can elevate another of John Gummer's contributions to the debate to the status of a doctrine: Gummer's Doctrine Number Two:

> We can argue about where to put the target, but the Commons must be united on the basis that the target is unconnected with our ability to deliver it, because it is forced upon us by the effects of climate change. To say otherwise would be like saying we will fight a war when we know we have enough guns, but in the meantime, if we are overrun, we cannot fight the war.[17]

I would prefer a different analogy: a patient is asked to accept major surgery, e.g. a leg amputation, but what's on offer will leave the job only 60% (or even 80% for that matter) complete – perhaps in order to allow the surgeon to get to his golfing date. Gummer's Doctrine No. 2 flies in the face of what the former government chief scientific advisor, Prof. Sir David King has often been criticised for, namely talking of a 'politically acceptable concentration level of GHGs in the atmosphere,' which could be in the mid-500s ppmv range. We know what he meant by 'political acceptability' – in blunt terms, an absence of political will – but should anything less be proffered as a solution? Doctrine No.2 combines measurability with necessity and all else is fudge.

Given that John Gummer chaired the Conservative Party's Quality of Life Commission, it could be assumed that he holds great sway over the future course of Conservative climate change policy. But ranged against him is the metaphorical golf-loving surgeon John Redwood whose pending golfing tournament is, so to speak the 'real politics' here. How they reconcile their differences will be indicative of whether 'science' will ever be a politically acceptable master, especially for a party which scents power just around the corner after a hard 13 years slog in the wilderness. The Conservative's urge to power may be too irresistible to allow the second of these doctrines is put in to practice.

The idea that a single political party may be capable all on its own of resolving the great problems of the day is one which has developed out of the left-right ideological dichotomy, which Tony Blair tried to overturn with his triangulating 'third way.' Triangulation was meant to free us of the narrow confines of ideology, but the alternative, intermittent 'third way' in practice leant largely towards freer markets and a 'choice' agenda which was a very reluctant companion to the public service ethos, given that it failed to differentiate between the real kinds of choices people make when they aren't blinded by consumerism. After the new Labour decade, and possibly following a realignment of official Conservativism beyond a 'compassionate charity' approach to the welfare state, there in reality is not that much of real substance dividing the parties. Markets, the role of the individual as a job seeker, the private sector role in education (e.g. academies) and health (polyclinics, or whatever path the Conservative policy takes), in defence (Trident replacement), in energy (nuclear: although the Conservatives stance on feed-in tariffs is more interventionist), in international development (forget our past record, we all want to reach the UN's development targets now), in trade (more liberalisation), in constitutional reform (we'll all abolish the Lords) – the Conservative list goes on. It may be a good thing in some of these areas if there is unanimity – for example, in maintaining pressure to honour the UN pledges on international development that were made nearly 40 years ago. But although policy convergence is a necessary condition of consensus, it is not sufficient. If we are to meet Gummer's Doctrines head-on, there has to be an acknowledgement that for a consensus to work there must be structures agreed which will cost any freeloader an immense amount of political capital. When the opposition parties' consensus agreement collapsed, it probably didn't do any of them very much harm, because nobody took it all that seriously in the first place.

My suggested starting point was expressed in an EDM launched in May, 2008:

> That this House notes the seriousness and urgency of climate change; calls upon the Prime Minister to convene a conference of the leaders of all parties represented in the UK Parliament, the Scottish Parliament and the Welsh Assembly to examine the formation of a cross-party consensus on climate change policy; and believes that all participants in such a conference should assent to there being no pre-conditions on their attendance.[18]

The EDM surprisingly won the support of two Conservative MPs, 21 Labour, four Liberal Democrats, two Plaid Cymru, one SNP and one independent MP – representatives from all sides of the House except the Democratic Ulster Unionists, but by July, 2005 still only 31 MPs in all.[19]

The first question MPs might ask is 'what are the conditions to there being no conditions?' The word 'unconditional' has often preceded another: 'surrender' and the implicit question is actually quite valid: what are you asking us to give up? The next question, which hardly needs saying, is 'what will the other side get out of this?' At this point, the most one might ordinarily hope for is a conclusion which leaves everybody's pride intact but succeeds in little else – a common enough outcome of difficult negotiations. Is it imaginable that we might see Gordon Brown and Alex Salmond in earnest conclave, or perhaps David Cameron and Nick Clegg? These are people who are professionally trained to distrust each other, and to do so with gusto on behalf of their parties – never mind how much we all agree with each other in the shadows of the Committee Corridor. Perhaps only a figure of trust – above the politicking but with constitutional authority – might be able to ensure such a convention could succeed, and that leaves us in the UK with only one choice – our head of state. This is not a debate about republicanism after all. And it might bring in the Ulster unionists (but not Sinn Fein, who in any case have not taken their seats in the Commons). The Monarch's role as defined by Walter Bagehot – "the right to be consulted, the right to encourage, the right to warn" could be critical to the success of a cross-party climate change convention.[20] Since the membership of such a convention would otherwise be composed entirely of parliamentarians, it would be hard to see how such a unique development could lead to fears that it was a breach of parliamentary privilege, though no doubt that would be a concern in some quarters. The importance of the head of state's contribution would be to stress the importance of the agenda, a matter to which the heir to the throne might also subscribe. There are of course many fears, not least on the left about what such a step may anticipate. The last time there was serious discussion about a new role for the royals – specifically Lord Mountbatten – it was in response to the perceived failings of the Wilson governments in the 1960s and 70s, and reflected extreme right-wing fears about a socialistic moral and economic malaise infecting the Kingdom. Talk of a coup lay near the surface.

Buried now not far below the surface of environmental consensus building is the skeleton of authoritarianism, which is not simply about a liberal horror at removing the 'democratic choice' between two policies, as Tony Benn seemed so astonished about in the 1970s – this is an authoritarianism which is more commonly and bitingly described as eco-fascism. Some of this concern arises from fears over population growth (always a sensitive subject in environmental debate and one which is often steered clear of). But eco-fascism can be a political and cultural home to those who reject the values of contemporary society and the following description of a formative twentieth century experience captures this mindset:

> It is striking how many traits the Wandervögel [an early twentieth century German youth group many of whose members went on to join the Nazis] have in common with the Deep Ecology movement. In particular, their self-conception that they were a "non-political" response to a deep cultural crisis, favoring direct emotional experience over social critique and action. . . Janet Biehl states, "When respect for nature comes to mean reverence, it can mutate ecological politics into a religion that 'Green Adolfs' can effectively use for authoritarian ends." In Britain, a wing of the National Front issues the cry,

"Racial preservation is Green!" while in the United States, white supremacist Monique Wolfing remarks that animals and the environment, "are in the same position as we are. Why would we want something created for ourselves and yet watch nature be destroyed? We work hand in hand with nature and we should save nature along with trying to save our race."[21]

An influential early environmentalist in the UK, Lord Lymington, active in the post-war period had views which

> . . centred around selective breeding, organic farming and a 'back to the soil' approach, with a strong emphasis in national self-sufficiency in food supply. During the period that Lymington was the most publicly known environmentalist in the UK, the organisations with which he was involved tended to avow the politics that were not far from the 'blut und boden' (blood and soil) ideas of the Third Reich.[22]

Lymington was a member of a group of people effectively acting as midwives to what would first become a political party called People, which went on to become the Ecology Party and finally became the Green Party. Clearly today's Green Party is far removed from the 'blut und boden' underpinnings of these earlier forms of environmentalism – any resemblance to a fascist party is laughable, given the problems the Green Party has had even deciding how many leaders it should have or in the policies it espouses today (a neat summary was given in the Guardian by the Green Party's first single leader, Caroline Lucas MEP on the 1st August 2008, e.g. opposing the Iraq war, promoting civil liberties, more equal income distribution and so on). But the authoritarian, populist appeal that a mutated form of environmentalism could make is obvious, when population issues are at its core. The Great Global Warming Swindle for example portrayed modern day environmentalists as an elite group prepared to keep the developing world in hunger by pursuing policies which would prevent their industrial development and thus their escape from poverty. A concomitant thread of the 'population explosion' is at least tied up with immigration concerns and more sinisterly, racism. One negative strand to the idea of self-sufficiency or even localism is that populations of other countries 'should look after themselves first and not come over here' regardless of what damage we may have inflicted historically and still inflict on their economies. This is a view which has a kind of mirror image in some circles in the developing world, but in that case turns it on its head the argument to demand reparations before dreaming of going any further – a stumbling block which almost certainly will be a step too far for the developed world in climate change negotiations.

The slightest taint of eco-fascism could be a major barrier to seeking a form of consensus politics which could be saleable to the public – on the one hand because of anti-democratic political impulses, or on the other for precisely the opposite reason if it delivered a populist message. The presentation of unwelcome radical policies in the former context could suffer from the brush of what inevitably some pundits would describe as 'extreme.' Indeed, an early usage of the word 'radical' in its political context was "one who holds the most advanced views of political reform on democratic lines, and thus belongs to the extreme section of the Liberal Party."[23] In 1802, our modern form of democracy would undoubtedly have looked extreme, and in 2008 it is perhaps hard to envisage what improvements could be made to it which would at least equal the changes that have occurred in the last two hundred years. Perhaps that's just a lack of imagination on the author's part, but the 'extremism' that may now challenge society could be the curtailment of democracy, or possibly the use of artificial democratic devices to give legitimacy to undemocratic behaviour – all in the name of the good of the people. On the road to such a society, we won't have wait long to hear its detractors, even if they don't believe it is fascism per se, but may be the next best thing, i.e. corporatism. In July, 2008, the New Economic Foundation had just published a report called A Green New Deal: joined-up policies to solve the triple crunch of the credit crisis, climate change and high oil prices. This would be a welcome miracle indeed, and it came with a bold wish to bring

> diverse social and industrial forces together, leading to a new progressive movement. We believe that our joint signatories point to an exciting possibility of a new political alliance: an alliance between the labour movement and the green movement, between those engaged in manufacturing and the public sector, between civil society and academia, industry, agriculture and those working productively in the service industries. [24]

One wonders where the right, or indeed those who are not 'working productively in the service industries' will fit in to the green new deal – re-employment in more useful occupations one hopes. The new green deal takes as one of its models Roosevelt's New Deal of the 1930s, and this could lead to the kind of the charge, ironically from the right, that was thrown at Roosevelt's legacy:

In the United States Republican President Ronald Reagan echoed Republican President Herbert Hoover and others who claimed that Franklin D. Roosevelt's New Deal programs represented a move in the direction of a corporatist state. These claims are highly disputed. In particular these critics focused on the National Recovery Administration. In 1935 Herbert Hoover described some of the New Deal measures as "Fascist regimentation." In his 1951 memoirs he used the phrases "early Roosevelt fascist measures", and "this stuff was pure fascism", and "a remaking of Mussolini's corporate state".[25]

These charges were pure nonsense of course, but they were little different in tone and meaning to Churchill's charge in the 1945 general election that Attlee's government in pursuance of its economic policies would probably have to set up some kind of Gestapo. The fact that A Green New Deal, alongside deserved admiration for Roosevelt's New Deal also cites in support of its remedies Cuba's response to the collapse of its oil supply after the fall of the Soviet Union will only instil in many the fear that these 'lefty-greens' are plotting something here which would tend towards authoritarianism, backed up with the full panoply of powers of a new corporatist state.

Overcoming this difficulty is the challenge the mainstream political parties face, more so than the smaller parties whose poverty of power is freedom; or, to put it another way it is the challenge the smaller parties face if they want to become mainstream and perhaps succeed in that goal even before they have the chance to scold the rest of us with an 'I told you so.'

Looking abroad for examples of cross-party consensus building brings up some surprising examples. In the United States congress, bills are brought forward with bi-partisan support. Hence the Lieberman-McCain bill (Climate Change and Stewardship), the Bingaman-Specter bill (Low Carbon Economy), the Fienstein-Carper bill (Electric Utility Cap and Trade) or the Olver-Gilchrest bill (Climate Stewardship) to mention but a few. Whilst the Republican and Democrat parties have a whipping system it is not as strong as in the UK – in elections, most candidates for Congress major on their personalities and their local successes count for a lot – e.g. how many 'boondoggles' they may have won for their home turf. In the words of former House Speaker Tip O'Neill, 'all politics is local.' Patronage thus plays a greater role, as does campaign finance, since members of Congress stand for election every two years. One can see the constraints representatives will have in pushing forward radical policies when vested interests exercise so much influence on individual politicians, and these pressures are very different to keeping to party manifestos as is the case for those seeking election in the UK. In this sense the US two party system is less of a straightjacket even though it firmly remains a two party system. In the context of putting private members bills forward, UK members of parliament nearly always seek cross party support, but this is in a legislature which generally limits the remit of such bills to minor matters (with one or two obvious exceptions such as abortion). In the UK, with no separation between the legislature and the executive, the government keeps a tight grip on what it is prepared to allow MPs legislate for. In the US far more bartering takes place between the legislature and the executive. It is not clear to me that either the British or American systems are superior to one or other, since both have serious flaws standing in the way of consensus building. Yet the bi-partisan presentation of bills in the US Congress suggests that for legislation to move ahead, quite a lot of testing across the divide has to take place first, although this rule seemed to apply a little less when Congress was called upon to deal with the economic crisis in 2007, with brief but very public cross party support for a $700 billion bail-out of Wall Street. President Bush, underlying the importance of the emergency legislation went so far as to call in both presidential candidates, like a re-run of an episode from the West Wing. No such urgency – some would say panic – has been accorded to tackling climate change, still less with the level of expenditure sought to help the banks out.

Perhaps parliaments elected on proportional representation systems offer more hope. In Denmark, with a permanent mix of smaller parties in Parliament, and agreement on energy efficiency was signed in 2003 which brought together all the parties of government and opposition. Whether the agreement was as radical as it could have been is debatable, but it did demonstrate a common purpose in some detail. In Germany, it cannot be denied that the influence of the Green Party, as a junior partner in Gerhard Schroeder's governments had a significant impact on environmental and particularly energy policies – aided by strong vices within the SPD like Hermann Scheer. Germany's commitment to keep to its commitment to phase out nuclear power owes much to this partnership, which employs a practical approach to renewable energy second to none in Europe. The SPD's non-nuclear commitment has remained after the formation of Angela Merkel's grand coalition between Christian Democrats and SPD, but with a general election coming up in 2009, the signs are that the Christian Democrats may rescind their support for the non-nuclear stance. Nevertheless, it is clear that whilst in coalition government Merkel has remained committed to the growth in renewable energy started by her predecessor, and this to a large extent is a testament to the worth of coalition politics. In Ireland too there now seems to be a fresh commitment to renewable energy, and once again this comes at a time when a coalition government has included green politicians.

Short of changing the electoral system, which in itself will not guarantee the implementation of climate change policies which are sufficient to the task, what else can be done in the short term to influence the political process? It was once said, though I cannot recall by whom, that a climate solution will be found either through a top-down process or a bottom-up process – or through catastrophe. Hoping that we may avoid the third option, and whilst desiring the first, there needs to be a more determined bottom-up process. Normal campaigning by Friends of the Earth, Greenpeace and all the other environmental NGOs, working in greater harmony with development NGOs (following the publication of their formative Up in Smoke report) has produced results, although trying to sift through all the claims for credit for the introduction of the Climate Change Bill can be a bit tiresome.[26] After the 2005 Gleneagles G8 summit and the impact of the Make Poverty History campaign (or was that: 'it was Bob wot won it' ?) came an effort by environmental and development groups to replicate the Make Poverty History strategy, by combining their effort and seeking to build a much larger and more influential critical mass in a campaign called Stop Climate Chaos. Three years later, this strategy does not seem to have worked. The reasons for this may be several – the absence of high profile cheerleaders perhaps, or because the problem it sought to address may actually be so complex that the solutions did not seem as easy as they were for 'making poverty history.' In that last regard, it is easy to see for example how Make Poverty History might attract the support of people who at the same time have no difficulty flying away on holidays. There could after all (we tell ourselves) be a case for eco-tourism, and jetting around the world is seen by some rightly or wrongly as one way of helping poor economies. But aside from that example there are plenty of conflicting messages about what it is good or bad to do to 'stop climate chaos' which thoroughly obfuscate the truth and drown out a clear-cut rallying call.

The efficacy of the usual tools of campaigning must also be questioned when time is running out. Petitions, demonstrations, postcard campaigns, letter-writing – all these things have their place, but to practised politicians they have – well, their place. In recent times London witnessed two of the largest demonstrations ever held in the UK, one protesting against the proposed ban on fox-hunting, the other against the Iraq war. Each had over a million participants but both were ignored by the government. Commentators would no doubt shrug their shoulders – 'that's typical of Tony Blair and new Labour' – but it is not so simple. I opposed the war but supported the fox hunting ban – should I change my mind because of a demonstration? But what if everybody joined the campaign, not a million but say 20 million? Then things might be different, but in the meantime for most protests in the streets, marchers will be outnumbered by the shoppers in Marks and Spencer on a Saturday afternoon. The voice or lack of it of the silent majority will, indeed in a democracy must - be heard too – which is to say life goes on. Traditional campaign methods should continue to be used for a variety of reasons – to inspire, to meet, to exchange ideas, but climate change is a problem which needs more than that after twenty years of ruminating indecision. It seems inescapable that the tactics of the fuel protestors in 2000, which had a noticeable impact on life and politics may become increasingly common, and in November 2008 the Observer was even, if somewhat tendentiously, reporting on 'eco-terrorists.' Tendentiously because the use of the word terrorist is now so broadly misused.

The political paradigm that we now operate under suggests that political parties have lost their appeal as activist organisations, succumbing as they have to vested interests, large media budgets, careerists and patronage. Their membership has plummeted as political activism has risen elsewhere. Thus, today's paradigm posits a small group of politicos surrounded by a larger group of mainly single issue activists, drawn to many causes who see their task as capturing the former group. But the politicos are far too sophisticated for that – having been trained in the broad church of representative democracy, their ability to play two wings to the centre rarely fails. There's nothing essentially wrong with that if it maintains stability and cohesion, but if it is the crowning glory of a democracy that is built on foundations of sand and hubristic self-denial, it may be an inappropriate peace. For their part, the single issue activists bring clear principles to their campaign, but politics is happier with compromise and an inevitable gap emerges between the two. No week goes by somewhere in the nation when some politician isn't accused of 'selling-out.' This chasm between two forms of political activism has to be bridged if those wielding power are to be rescued from their sclerotic self-content and those outside from their piety.

One approach worth exploring, but which deservedly got a bad name (at least in the Labour Party in the 1980s) is entryism. Practised most successfully for a period by the Trotskyist Militant Tendency, the objective is to take over an organisation through infiltration. At the local level – where Militant had its greatest successes – this means taking control of branches and party organisations, controlling meeting agendas and where necessary simply wearing out internal opposition. Through entryism into the Labour Party, Militant eventually and notoriously won control of Liverpool City Council, had many councillors elected elsewhere and won a handful of parliamentary seats under the guise of the Labour banner. For those who had to put up with Militant it was an unpleasant experience, but their strategy demonstrably worked until a new Labour leader, Neil Kinnock determined to stamp out entryism in the party. The membership of political parties today is much smaller than twenty years ago – with today perhaps no more than 600,000 between them all. Were a significant number of environmentalists to swallow their pride and join those parties, or at least the ones which may stand a chance of forming the next government, they may exercise more influence than any other method, especially if they were organised and needless to say, disciplined around common objectives. Entryism does have sinister connotations – Militant is not a healthy looking precedent – but what political party today would want to turn away new members who speak the language of Red/Green, Blue/Green or Yellow/Green? Green/Green is a language which like Esperanto ought to be universal, but like Esperanto remains the preserve of the few.

In the meantime, the Stop Climate Chaos campaign appears to have become becalmed and a new movement seems to be developing around direct action. This takes several forms and builds upon the well-trodden roads of direct action movements in the past, be they shareholder activism and boycotts during the apartheid era, or attempts at blockading offending sites a la Greenham Common. How one judges the success of those campaigns varies and no doubt lessons can be learnt from them but they mainly had one thing in common, namely that the target of change was separate from those seeking the change. Climate change poses a categorically different target – we ourselves are the target alongside the energy companies, governments and others who perpetuate the carbon economy. This thought stuck me forcefully when returning from the Climate Camp at Kingsnorth, Kent in August, 2008. It was already dark and the streets were lit, homes were lit, TVs were on, and kettles were no doubt boiling in kitchens (a few days later, watching Andrew Marr's Britain from Above, I learnt that when Eastenders comes to a close each night the national grid can expect anything up to a 2GW power demand surge as people go to make their cups of tea).

The 'need' to build a new coal-fuelled power plant at Kingsnorth is therefore entirely dependent on the demand for its product - electricity. If there were no demand, there would be no new Kingsnorth. But Kingsnorth is impersonal, and as much as I support the campaign to prevent a new coal power station being built (especially as it will be built without any means of capturing its carbon dioxide emissions) it is only by addressing society's electricity consumption that the immediate carbon footprint of the UK energy sector could be reduced, to allow time for renewable energy to replace fossil fuels. It is conceivable that 1,500 campaigners could close down a Kingsnorth or a Drax, but not for long, and not very often. And if the result were power cuts, would the mass population rally to the cause – or ring the police asking for tougher action to stop more black-outs?

Whatever the answer to that question, there is enormous value in the Climate Camp's organisers' approach, since it does help the media focus on the story (always provided it is not too clouded by issues of excessive policing – which I saw with my own eyes at Kingsnorth). The real story is that whilst our current energy system remains vulnerable, as it is, it inevitably makes us vulnerable – to more than just the lights going off. But what must campaigners do to be successful, if we are to steer the politics of climate change on to a swift, effective course? At a workshop at the camp, hopes were pinned on what might happen at the UNFCCC COP15 climate change conference in Copenhagen in December, 2009, and one proposition posed at the very beginning of the meeting was that the delegates to the COP15 talks should be imprisoned in their conference hall until they produced something of value. The suggestion was made by one whose Marxist analysis would have found favour in any Socialist Workers Party meeting, and intentionally or not it illustrated precisely how utterly resistant to reductionism the issue of climate change is – not least for the poor UNFCCC delegates who may find themselves sleeping on the Copenhagen conference hall floor if some protestors have anything to do with it. One wonders whether we should expect a Kyoto Two or a Copenhagen One to have the slightest chance of addressing the system which gives rise to the inexorable push for fossil fuels in the first place. Is the delegate from Kenya or those others of poorer G77 countries, who do not bear responsibility for climate change to be imprisoned too in order to learn how they are the underdogs in a capitalist system? That would be to say the least, counterproductive.

It may well be possible to shut down a conference, or trap the delegates, or expose it all as a sham – but where does that leave us? Many of those who were at the ill-fated WTO conference in Seattle in 1999 could cite that occasion as an example of the impact of disruptive direct action on the culture of summits – the onward march of the WTO stumbled and tripped – but what did that eventually do for the unemployed of Africa? How were the demands of the protestors actually related to the demands of the hungry in the developing world when it came to delivering a result? The Kingsnorth climate camp workshop I attended raised more questions than it answered, and politically the question that refused to go away was: how do our tactics deliver our strategy? And by the way, what is our strategy? Somehow, it has to include getting all those kettle-fillers on board. Strikingly, this uncertainty which manifested itself at the Climate Camp has a perfect mirror image in government policy. There are no prizes for guessing which exhibition of uncertainty poses the greater threat.

Notes

1. http://obama.senate.gov/speech/060403-energy_independ/index.php
2. Tony Benn, *Against the Tide, Diaries 1973-76* Hutchinson, London, 1989, p.84
3. Edward Heath, *The Course of My Life,* Hodder and Stroughton, London 1998 p.506
4. Environmental Audit Committee
5. *Times,* 31st October 2005
6. Hansard 18th May 2006
7. Climate Change Programme, Defra, 2006
8. see Annex One in the All Party Parliamentary Climate Change Group report, Westminster 2006 for full text
9. Nick Hurd MP and Clare Kerr, *Don't Give Up On 2°,* Conservative Party Quality of Life Commission, 2006 p.4
10. www.conservatives.com/tile.do?def=safer.greener.page
11. *Evening Standard,* 16th June 2008
12. *Yorkshire Post,* 29th May 2008
13. *Evening Standard,* op cit
14. Hurd and Kerr, op cit
15. One of the most consistent and well informed opponents of the use of carbon markets has been the NGO Cornerhouse, whose work should be given more parliamentary attention.
16. Official Report, Climate Change Bill [Lords] Tuesday 24th June Col.10
17. ibid col. 70
18. Early Day Motion 1636 22nd May 2008
19. This was my fault for not including, through an unpardonable oversight mention of the Northern Ireland Assembly in my EDM. But co-incidentally in partial mitigation I plead that my attention was drawn to an article in the July/August edition of *Energy in Buildings and Industry* magazine to what DUP MP Sammy Wilson said after voting against the Climate Change Bill that "the reason behind the Bill is this fixation that somehow, whether if you reduce carbon dioxide emissions, you will change the world's climate. There is absolutely no

consensus that this is the case. Two hundred years ago people were skating on the Thames and there was a mini-Ice Age. One thousand years ago there were grapes grown in Scotland. There have always been cycles in the Erath's climate. And they have little or nothing to do with man's activities." Mr Wilson also serves as the Environment Minister in Northern Ireland's executive.

20. (http://www.royal.gov.uk/output/page4682.asp)
21. *Ecofascism: Deep Ecology and Right-Wing Co-optation by Kev Smith, Greenpepper* http://www.greens.org/s-r/32/32-13.html
22. Simon Matthews *Kiss me on the apocalypse! Some reflections on the life, times and politics of Sir James Goldsmith*, Lobster, Summer 2008 Hull p 34
23. The Shorter Oxford English Dictionary, 1973
24. nef, London July 2008
25. http://en.wikipedia.org/wiki/Corporatism#Criticism_of_Corporatism
26. *Up in Smoke: threats form and responses to the impact of global warming on human development*, Up in Smoke coalition of NGOs, London, October 2005

epilogue

It would be ironic indeed if the 2008/09 recession provided the inspiration for a new political will to tackle climate change, with a rush to invest in green technologies as a way of revitalising commerce. Of course this would be welcome so far as it goes and some commentators may ask who cares how we get there, so long as the effort is made. To be totally cynical, we could add for good measure that during the recession we will inevitably witness a significant drop in GHG emissions as consumption declines. At a later date, political leaders will be able to point to such a reduction – as the Bush administration once did – as proof of their successful climate change policies. There lies the danger, for when –and if - our economic woes are safely behind us might we simply return (yet again) to business as usual?

Just as the global financial system has lately been subject to considerable high level political attention as a consequence of the exposure to its inherent instability, a similar exercise – at the political level - urgently needs to be carried out on the sustainability of the planet's biosphere. In fact much of the preparatory work has been done, not just by the IPCC but also in 2005, when the report of the UN Millennium Ecosystem Assessment (MEA) was published. This described ecosystems as services which benefit people such as food, water or climate regulation. That's not a description of nature which everyone would concur with but one rooted in actuality. Surveying 24 such services, the MA found 15 were degraded or being exhausted. Of the remaining nine ecosystem services, five reported some sustainability and some degradation. The four that had improved were food (crops, livestock and aquaculture) and global climate regulation (in terms of a net increase in carbon sequestration since the mid-nineteenth century).[1] And what was in decline? Water, soil erosion, pest regulation, pollination and natural defences against natural hazards to name but a few. With such degradation, one might be tempted to ask how truly sustainable our food ecosystems are, and whether recent improvements in productivity will continue at sufficient pace to feed a growing population. The MEA has given us the clearest insight yet as to how fragile our natural 'banking' system is – how close to bankruptcy it is – but because as yet it has proven resilient enough, with literally and figuratively speaking ever higher doses of fertiliser, it has been relegated to secondary status whilst the shattered nerves of financiers and speculators are mended with what could be a tonic worth trillions of dollars.

No clearer sign of our continuing inability to change course is the establishment's reaction to the economic crisis. There has been much talk of greening the economy, and undeniably there will be some substance in that. But the main thrust has been to return to growth through restoring consumer confidence. There is nothing original or new in this, indeed it is exactly what George W. Bush decreed in the early 2000s recession. The headline writers at the Financial Times could have simply dusted down some of their old work when in November 2008 their front page lead was 'UK urged to shop its way out of crisis.'[2] How can this approach be made compatible with our objective to cut greenhouse gas emissions? Every year Defra produces a handy booklet called 'Sustainable development indicators in your pocket.' For the first time in 2008, it showed the estimated level of carbon emissions 'associated with goods and services consumed in the UK.'[3] So whilst the same booklet reveals that between 1990 and 2007 UK domestically produced greenhouse gas emissions declined by 17% on the standard Kyoto measure (which excludes aviation and shipping but includes carbon offsets purchased overseas), the truer measure including all emissions relating to activity in the UK rose by 18% between 1992 and 2004 (and one might reasonably expect that figure to be higher if we were comparing it to the same period of the original narrower measure, i.e. 1990 to 2007).

There is no clearer sign that we are blind to our predicament, just as we were wilfully blind to the development of a sub-prime economy. My colleagues might lambast me for saying this. After all, haven't we seen the UK introduce the world's first greenhouse gas reduction targets and the world's first legally mandated carbon budgets ? Well yes, we have, and these are positive steps towards a fuller comprehension of the problem, even if we are not yet willing the means to accomplish the scale of change required. Whilst Faustus thought he still had time to reflect and cogitate, and despite knowing what was the right thing to do - he was a thoughtful man after all - he nevertheless took the advice of the Bad Angel rather than the Good one and continued with his 24-year binge. Only when it was too late did he suddenly get serious. So, in the limited confines of classical economic practice, the only answer to our conked-out consumer binge is to try to resuscitate it with an injection of taxpayer's money - £12.5 billion in lost VAT receipts to secure a 2½% consumption tax reduction – almost equivalent to 1% of GDP, i.e. nearly the same as Nick Stern's original costing of dealing with climate change, and more recently the lower end of the price put on it by the independent Climate Change Committee chaired by Adair Turner. I think it is safe to assume the climate change opportunity cost of this loss in VAT receipts is going to be much greater than 1%. If it means we can suck in more Chinese goods, produced at a greater cost in greenhouse gas emissions, we will have to spend even more to put right the damage.

Less is more needs to become our new political Hippocratic oath. To use less whilst we still have the choice as a society to make this collective decision, rather than have it forced upon us by harsh reality is merely common sense. We have the technologies to wean ourselves off fossil fuels, but not the political will to stand up to the vested interests who fret over their market share, shareholder value, sunk costs and profit margins. We have the capacity to make things last longer and discard less, but we have such a materialist definition of self esteem, relatively few are willing to contemplate any other way. This is not an anti-materialist philosophy, but a call for a re-evaluation of the actual worth of things, taking on board the concept of all an object's externalities, whether environmental or social.

As a member of the Labour Party (and a long-standing one at that) I have always understood the core values of the Party to be rooted in social justice. Tackling human poverty and inequality were the ambitions of the founders of the party and its reason for being. Now we must understand that these values cannot operate in the absence of a globally integrated framework, a framework based not on a purely social model, but a socio-environmental model. We are told we live in a 'globalised world' (sic) but still cling to behaviour which does not integrate globalisation in its fullest sense. Thus trade policy and climate change policy remain at loggerheads in a battle between greater global consumption and climate change mitigation. Anyone who claims that we are genuinely getting to grips with squaring this circle is living in cloud cuckoo land.

Less is more is also a complete riposte to those who believe that environmentalists are a bunch of grumbling miseries who want everyone to wear hair-shirts. This stereotypical dismissal of those who talk of sustainability doesn't bear scrutiny of course, but is made all the more wearisome when it comes from the mouths of people whose only concept of a natural cycle is boom and bust economics. The message that has to be conveyed now by anyone interested in social justice is that it cannot be obtained without integrating the concepts of environmentalism. Social justice is only going to happen if there is more equity across the globe – the model of social justice which we by and large pursued in the past was, to coin a phrase, merely 'social justice in one country'. Globalisation dispatched that luxury to the history books.

Thus the climate change challenge is an opportunity as well as a threat but only if the solutions put forward form part of an integrated pathway which shows all people, wherever they live, how their contribution and share of the burden fits in with everybody else's. A ragbag of projects stitched together and called a framework, however well-intentioned will not suffice. The excluded would never accept it and worse they may see it as a license to carry on as before – the same argument that is used regularly by those who oppose the Tobin Tax on currency transactions now makes the case for an inclusive climate change deal.

So, following on from that, if I were to draw three things from this book, they are as follows:

First, let's recognise that a global deal has to be fully inclusive, demonstrate how we calculate burden sharing and be equitable (no-one will accept a deal that builds in their disadvantage). That framework is Contraction and Convergence.

Second, the tension between democracy and consumerism has to be resolved: not by detached 'upstream' markets which few people understand but by the elector/consumer assuming choice and responsibility, with lots of assistance from the state and markets. We cannot wait upon a technological solution – behavioural change now is the 'bridging loan' to the future. People have to be given the power and the tools to control their own carbon emissions – personal carbon allowances are the obvious means of achieving this. We are perfectly capable of running reward cards, and in the same way personal carbon allowances should not be seen as some horrendous imposition but a route to lower energy costs, better public transport and all the other 'goods' that are so often talked up but delayed in the delivery. Consumer power should be harnessed not feared.

Third, to help achieve the above, the massive global subsidies to fossil fuels (which are supposed to be cheaper than renewables, remember) running in the order of $240 billion per year should be switched to energy efficiency projects and renewables (the latter currently receives just $38 billion).

These three steps – pretty big ones, I admit – would help move us away from climate change catastrophe and support a lifestyle with wich we could all be comfortable. Increasingly, the opposition to these approaches will come from die-hard fossil fuel junkies. The trouble is – and let's be honest - that's pretty much all of us.

Notes

1. United Nations Millennium Ecosystems Assessment at http://www.millenniumassessment.org/en/index.aspx
2. Financial Times, 27th November 2008
3. Defra, London 2008

bibliography

Brown, Lester R., *Plan B2.0: Rescuing a Planet Under Stress and a Civilisation in Trouble*, Norton, New York 2006

Caster, Neil, *The politics of the environment: Ideas, Activism, Policy*, Cambridge University Press, Cambridge, 2007

Cline, William R., *The Economics of Global Warming*, Institute for International Economics, Washington 1992

Cromwell, David and Levene, Mark (eds)., *Surviving Climate Change: the struggle to avert global catastrophe*, Pluto, London 2007

Dessler, Andrew E. and Parson, Edward A., *The Science and Politics of Global Climate Change: A guide*, Cambridge University Press, Cambridge 2006

Douthwaite, Richard, *The Growth Illusion, How economic growth has enriched the few, impoverished the many and endangered the planet*, Lilliput Press, Dublin 1992

Flannery, Tim, *The Weathermakers: our changing climate and what it means for life on earth*, Penguin, London, 2007

Friedman, Thomas L., *Hot, Flat and Crowded: Why the world needs a green revolution - and how we can renew our global future*, Allen Lane, London 2008

Garnaut, Ross, The Garnaut Climate Change Review, Cambridge University Press, Cambridge 2008

Gore, Al, *An Inconvenient Truth*, Bloomsbury, London, 2006

Helm, Dieter (ed)., *Climate Change Policy*, Oxford University Press, Oxford 2005

Hillman, Meyer and Fawcett, Tina, *How we can save the planet*, Penguin, London 2004

Leggett, Jeremy, *The Carbon War: Dispatches from the end of the oil century*, Allen Lane, London 1999

Leggett, Jeremy, *Half-gone: Oil, Gas, Hot Air and the Global Energy Crisis*, Portobello, London 2005

Lovelock, James, *The Revenge of Gaia*, Penguin, London 2007

Meyer, Aubrey, *Contraction and Convergence: The Global Solution to Climate Change*, Green Books, Dartington, 2000

Mobbs, Paul, *Energy Beyond Oil*, Matador, Leicester 2005

Monbiot, George, *Heat: How to stop the planet from burning*, Allen Lane, London 2006

Newell, Peter, *Climate for Change: Non state actors and the global politics of the greenhouse*, Cambridge University Press, Cambridge 2000

O'Riordan, Tim and Jäger, Jill, *Politics of Climate Change – a European Perspective*, Routledge, London 1996

Paterson, Walt, *Keeping the Lights on: Towards Sustainable Electricity*, Earthscan, London 2007

Pearce, Fred, *When the Rivers Run Dry*, Eden Project Books, 2006

Saul, John Ralston, *The Unconscious Civilisation*, Anansi, Ontario 1995

Scheer, Hermann, *Energy Autonomy*, Earthscan, London 2006

Schellnhuber, Hans Joachim et al (eds)., *Avoiding Dangerous Climate Change*, Cambrdige University Press, Cambridge 2006

Simms, Andrew, *Ecological Debt: The health of the planet and wealth of nations*, Pluto, London 2005

Simms, Andrew and Smith, Jow (eds)., *Do Good Lives Have to Cost the Earth?* Constable, London 2008

Stern, Nicholas, *The Economics of Climate Change: The Stern Review*, Cambridge University Press, Cambridge, 2007

Stiglitz, Joseph and Blimes, *The Three Trillion Dollar War: the true cost of the Iraq conflict*, Allen Lane, London 2008

Walker, Gabrielle and King, Sir David, *The Hot Topic: How to tackle global warming and still keep the lights on*, Bloomsbury, London 2008

Wolmar, Christian, *Fire and Steam: A New History of the Railways in Britain*, Atlantic Books, London 2007

appendix: the All Party Parliamentary Climate Change Group (APPCCG)

The APPCCG, one of over a hundred parliamentary cross-party subject groups, was formed in 2005 and now has around 200 MPs and peers in membership, as well as having over 200 associate members, including businesses, academia, NGOs and individuals. The APPCCG enables parliamentarians with a shared interest in climate change to learn more about the subject, to meet with non-parliamentarians and to find ways of raising the political profile of the issue.

The APPCCG has:

- Launched a campaign (the 25/5 Campaign) to get parliamentarians to reduce their personal carbon emissions by 25% within five years. Over 60 MPs signed up.

- Instigated an inquiry to ask whether a cross party consensus on climate change was possible or desirable. The report was published in 2007.

- Hosted meetings with Al Gore and Mikhail Gorbachev amongst many other distinguished speakers.

- Launched an Anglo-German Parliamentary Partnership on Climate Change and Energy, which seeks to share and extend knowledge on successful approaches to these issues.

- Financially supported African NGO representation at the UNFCCC.

If you are interested in associate membership of the APPCCG and wish to participate in our meetings and activities, please contact the APPCCG Secretariat for more details:

APPCCG Secretariat
The CarbonNeutral Company
Bravington House
2 Bravington Walk
Regent Quarter
Kings Cross
London
N1 9AF

index